SPECTRUM OF PROTESTANT BELIEFS

Spectrum of Protestant Beliefs

Edited by REV. ROBERT CAMPBELL, O.P.

De Paul University

Contributors

DR. WILLIAM HAMILTON
Professor of Religion
New College

DR. CARL F. H. HENRY
Editor, Christianity Today

DR. BOB JONES, JR.
President, Bob Jones University

DR. JOHN WARWICK MONTGOMERY
Chairman, Church History Division
Trinity Evangelical Divinity School

BISHOP JAMES A. PIKE
Theologian-in-residence
Center for the Study of Democratic Institutions

THE BRUCE PUBLISHING COMPANY / Milwaukee

Library of Congress Catalog Card Number: 68–17118

Preface

This *Spectrum of Protestant Beliefs* has evolved through an attempt to present to Catholics a picture of Protestantism as it exists in America today. Most Catholics are quite unaware that the significant divisions in Protestantism no longer are along denominational lines, but rather depend on the orientation of the individual in the liberal-conservative spectrum. The average Protestant layman seems not much better informed. This presentation hopefully will be of assistance in giving Protestants as well as Catholics a more up-to-date picture of American Protestant attitudes and beliefs.

The left-to-right spectrum has been divided into five bands which seem most closely to represent the reality of the situation: radical, liberal, confessional, new evangelical, and fundamentalist. An outstanding spokesman from each of these bands was asked to make a statement on each of twenty-two key topics illustrating the religious, moral, and political attitudes prevailing in his band of the spectrum.

Representing the fundamentalist position is Bob Jones, Jr., for the past quarter-century president of thriving Bob Jones University in Greenville, South Carolina. Bob Jones University is regarded as a stronghold of fundamentalist education in the United States. Dr. Jones is the author of several books, including *Wine of Morning*, and *Ancient Truths for Modern Days*.

Speaking for the new evangelicals is Carl F. H. Henry, editor of the outstanding evangelical magazine, *Christianity Today*. Author of many books and editor of several more, Dr. Henry was the organizer of the World Congress on Evangelism in Berlin in 1966.

Dr. John Warwick Montgomery, Ph.D. from the University of Chicago and Th.D. from the University of Strasbourg, France, is chairman of the division of church history at Trinity Evangelical Divinity School in Deerfield, Illinois. He has contributed articles to numerous theological journals; among his books are *The Shape of the Past*, *The 'Is God Dead' Controversy*, and *Crisis in Lutheran Theology*. Dr. Montgomery speaks from the confessional segment of the spectrum.

Bishop James A. Pike is well known as an articulate spokesman for liberal positions on many controversial questions. Dr. Pike is theologian-in-residence at the Center for the Study of Democratic Institutions, Santa Barbara, and serves as a "worker-priest in the purple" of the Episcopal Diocese of California, of which he was until recently the Ordinary. Among his books are *The Faith of the Church*, *A Time for Christian Candor*, *What Is This Treasure?*, *You and the New Morality*, and most recent, *If This Be Heresy*.

Radical theologian William Hamilton, professor of religion at New College, Sarasota, Florida, rivals Thomas J. J. Altizer in being the foremost exponent of the "death-of-God" movement. He is co-author with Altizer of *Radical Theology and the Death of God* and author of *The New Essence of Christianity* and other works.

Introduction

"Frankly, I feel closer to a liberal of any denomination than I do to to a conservative of my own denomination," confessed the prominent Lutheran pastor of liberal views. "With a liberal of any persuasion, Presbyterian, Methodist or even Catholic, I find that we agree amazingly on important religious and moral and social issues, but with a conservative Lutheran — or any other kind of conservative — I just don't get along. It seems just impossible for us to have any dialogue whatsoever."

At the other end of the Protestant spectrum, the fundamentalists voice the same conclusion in reverse. "I don't care what denomination a man is, as long as he is a solid Bible Christian and has a saving faith in the Lord Jesus. With that man, I can have Christian fellowship. But the liberals have betrayed the Gospel. And the liberals of my own Baptist denomination are just as bad as the rest. Worse, because they should know better. Denying the deity of Christ, denying the Virgin Birth, denying the inspiration of the Scriptures — how can these modernists still claim to be Christians?"

This cleavage shows up in almost every Protestant denomination, a vast chasm which no man can cross fixed between Methodist and Methodist, between Baptist and Baptist, between Presbyterian and Presbyterian, between Lutheran and Lutheran. Parenthetically, observers are pointing out that this same "sub-surface schism" is appearing in the Roman Catholic Church.

The unbridgeable ideological gulf between the left and

the right in each denomination far exceeds the difference between denominations. Old-time Methodist-Baptist squabbles about baptism of infants or only of those who have accepted Christ are now dwarfed into insignificance by within-the-family divisions over the Virgin Birth; Calvinist-Arminian disputes over predestination and free will are pushed aside by liberal-fundamentalist disagreements about the Trinity and the literal interpretation of Scripture. The denunciations no longer are inter-denominational but intra-denominational. Even the Scopes trial is not dead; the battle continues within most denominations, but a battle in which the estrangement between right and left is so complete that neither hears, much less feels, the shots fired by the opposition.

Close observers of the Protestant scene have long been aware of this fact that denominations are becoming less significant in predicting the religious, moral, and political stance of an individual Protestant. How then can we arrive at a more meaningful grouping? The following fivefold division of the Protestant liberal-conservative spectrum was arrived at after many discussions with Protestant ministers of all persuasions. It seems to fit best the reality of the situation. However, it must be borne in mind that these groupings are approximations and that not every Protestant will fit neatly into one of the categories. The hand-in-hand affinity of religious and political conservatism — or liberalism — indicated by the opinions of the spokesmen in the following pages is the rule, but there are many exceptions. Former Vice-President Richard Nixon, Quaker, is liberal in his doctrinal views but conservative in political orientation. On the other hand, semi-fundamentalist Senator Mark Hatfield annoys his co-religionists and delights liberals by denouncing the "U. S. war of aggression in Vietnam."

This pioneering effort at a realistic grouping of popular Protestant attitudes may have overlooked some significant segment. If this is so, it is hoped that reader reaction will make this evident. Some might wish to put the Pentecostal* movement into a separate grouping. However it seems fair to classify them as fundamentalists inasmuch as they have all the beliefs and attitudes of that group, adding an emphasis on faith healing and speaking in tongues. It might also be asked why there was no inclusion of what might be called "developmental theology" — Martin E. Marty, Robert Mc- Afee Brown, Jaroslav Pelikan, etc. It was felt that these highly esteemed writers represent an articulate segment of publishing theologians but their views are not typical of a large identifiable segment of popular Protestant beliefs and attitudes. Perhaps reader reaction will dictate otherwise.

The Catholic reader will find that the attitudes attributed here to liberal Protestantism usually are quite congenial to the liberal Catholic, but the criterion here assigned for the liberal Protestant, non-acceptance of the Virgin Birth in the traditional sense, would not apply to the liberal Catholic, the great majority of whom accept the Catholic Church's teaching on the Virgin Birth. Therefore, if this test were applied to the liberal Catholic, he would qualify as a con- servative.

The average Protestant church member probably would not know offhand into which of the bands of the spectrum he fits best. But given a description of the bands, he should be able to locate his ideological position.

---

* This refers to the organized Pentecostal churches, not to the tiny glossalalia groups springing up in all denominations.

Contents

SPECTRUM OF PROTESTANT BELIEFS

Description of
Each Band of the Spectrum

FUNDAMENTALISM

The fundamentalist is characterized by a great devotion to the Bible and its inerrancy, by orthodoxy concerning basic Christian doctrines, and a conviction that salvation is by faith alone. He rejects all biblical criticism, and a literal interpretation of Scripture leads him to deny the theory of evolution. He has a strong belief in the traditional Christian teaching about heaven and hell, the divinity of Jesus Christ, the Trinity, Virgin Birth of Jesus, his atoning death on the cross, his Resurrection and Ascension into heaven. The Glock-Stark survey shows a higher percentage of orthodoxy on these doctrines among members of fundamentalist groups than obtains among members of other Protestant groups or even among Catholics. Fundamentalists also stress the Second Coming of Jesus Christ, preach it frequently, and many consider this return to be imminent.

Fundamentalists lay great emphasis on salvation by faith alone. Once a man has accepted Jesus Christ as his personal Savior, he is regenerated, born again, saved. Good works do not help toward salvation, but the man who has sincere faith will live a good life. Salvation is accomplished here and now, and the good works follow as a result, not vice versa as the Catholic and Orthodox and some Protestant groups teach.

Opposition to any collaboration in religious matters with those who they believe have not been true to the Bible leads the fundamentalists to denounce the ecumenical movement. In justification of their separatist attitudes, they offer the scriptural injunction of God to his people: "Come out and be a separate people."

This same attitude leads them to look with disfavor upon "worldly amusements," dancing, movies, card playing. A concern for the health of the body as temple of the Holy Spirit is the source of their customary avoidance of alcohol and tobacco.

The fundamentalist is very zealous to "lead others to Christ." One of his foremost concerns is to help others to accept Jesus Christ as Savior. He generously supports the many foreign missionaries sent out by his group. He is an ardent churchgoer, often twice a week, and gives a larger part of his income to the church than does his liberal counterpart. Most of his social life is built around the church. His friends are fellow church members and his entertainments are church socials. He is much concerned about the threat of communism, both domestic and foreign, and often considers the Catholic Church as dangerous a threat to America as is communism. He usually has less formal education than the more liberal Protestant.

NEW EVANGELICAL

The new evangelical has been called "a fundamentalist with a Ph.D." In basic Christian doctrine, he has the same strong faith as the fundamentalist and agrees in insisting on the total inspiration of the Bible. Parting company with the fundamentalist on a crucial issue, some new evangelicals believe "the inerrancy of the Bible in scientific matters is debatable; it was not intended as a scientific textbook. And perhaps our concept of inspiration needs more cautious definition."

The new evangelical is more ready to cooperate in interfaith dialogue with liberal Protestants and Catholics. The foremost new evangelical, Billy Graham, has been denounced by the foremost fundamentalist, Bob Jones, Jr., as "doing more harm to the cause of Christ than any other man."

This criticism springs largely from Graham's semi-ecumenical actions of appearing on the same platform with liberals and Catholics.

The typical member of this group is vigorously opposed to communism, liberalism and Catholicism, but usually does not denounce them in such strong terms as does the fundamentalist. Other characteristics of the fundamentalist apply to the new evangelical in a somewhat diluted form.

CONFESSIONAL

Contrasting to the "We have no creed but the gospel" attitude of the fundamentalists is the concern shown by "high church" Episcopalians and some Lutherans, notably Missouri Synod, for close adherence to a "confession of faith." The authoritative statement of church doctrine in the Apostles' Creed or Nicene Creed or in their own denominational confession of faith is considered by them to be the safest guide to the basic message of the Bible. This tradition considers the ecclesiastical organization to be a thing of much more authority and importance than do the fundamentalists or new evangelicals. In the latter two groups, congregations are more likely to be autonomous than among the ecclesially-oriented confessional group.

Going hand in hand with this is a greater concern for the liturgy. The worship service follows a set ritual, often with many similarities to the Catholic Mass. Altars and vestments lend a richness of color not found in the simplicity of the fundamentalist or new evangelical service.

Owing to a greater Continental influence, the confessional groups customarily do not have the same aversion to smoking, drinking, dancing and movies found among the fundamentalists, and to a lesser extent among the new evangelicals.

Doctrinally, confessional Protestants cover the spectrum from center to right: some are highly orthodox, accepting such key points of high orthodoxy as the reality of Satan and the Second Coming of Christ; others question this or that traditional doctrine, and some verge on a rejection of the physical reality of the Virgin Birth of Christ. Rejection of this would locate a person in the liberal camp. Politically the confessional person might be anywhere on the spectrum, but probably the majority tend to be conservative.

LIBERAL

Here the term liberal is defined as a Protestant church member who does not accept the doctrine of the Virgin Birth in the traditional sense, namely that Jesus Christ had no human father but was conceived by the Holy Spirit and born of a virgin — physically a virgin as well as in any figurative sense. This criterion for the liberal group was chosen because the Virgin Birth has long been an outstanding source of division in Protestant opinion. The recent Glock and Stark survey states that on the Virgin Birth "startling differences can be observed among the Protestant bodies." The Protestant who does not accept the Virgin Birth will a *fortiori* reject the traditional concepts of Satan, hell, the Second Coming of Christ. Some go further and challenge the traditional doctrines of the divinity of Christ and the Trinity.

The liberal is not so concerned about life after death as are the three groups to the right. Customarily, he expresses the attitude that the concept of personal immortality leaves him a little cool. "Let's live one life at a time and devote ourselves to building a better world right here." He considers the Bible to be highly figurative and symbolic in its language. Such things as the miracles of Christ are regarded as having purely natural explanations.

The religious liberal usually is politically liberal, too. He is enthusiastic about the civil rights movement and social welfare programs. Often he is strongly opposed to U. S. presence in Vietnam. The publications of this group are vigorous crusaders for liberal political causes. However, there seems to be a strong minority among the laity who are politi-

1. The Concept of God

I. JONES

I believe in a triune God — Father, Son, and Holy Spirit. The Bible tells us that God is Love. There are many facets to the jewel of His character — righteousness, holiness, truth, etc. You could name them all day; but His very nature is love. Because God is Love, He sent His Son to earth to die for man's sin. God is infinitely perfect in all of His ways, so holy that He cannot overlook sin; and it was necessary that sin's penalty be paid on the cross in order for man, the sinner, to be reconciled to the sinless God.

II. HENRY

God is the self-revealing supernatural source, support, and end of all things, the sovereign Creator of the universe and of man in His moral image for fellowship with Himself, the holy Judge of the universe, and the Redeemer of all who put their obedient trust in Him. He is manifested universally in nature and history, and even in the rebellious conscience of fallen man, and has inspired the scriptural revelation as an intelligible, objective disclosure of Himself and of His works and words. He is infinite in knowledge and wisdom, righteousness and justice, power and sovereignty, and goodness and love. Unchanging in His being, He is one God self-disclosed in three eternal personal centers of consciousness, Father, Son, and Holy Spirit.

9

III. Montgomery

I liked the recent "dialogue" between Gabriel and God in *Presbyterian Life:*

> *Gabriel.* I swear-uh-state unequivocally that some young theologians are saying that your Primordial Totality has metamorphosed into the epiphany of immanence.
> *God.* What does that mean?
> *Gabriel.* I don't know, but we've got Augustine working on it.
> *God.* Is brother Beelzebub behind this?
> *Gabriel.* Actually, it started when a philosopher named Nietzsche coined the phrase, "God is dead" —
> *God.* What is he doing now?
> *Gabriel.* He's just finished writing on the west wall, "I was wrong" three trillion times.

To claim that "God is dead" is to be at least three trillion times wrong, for if God did not exist the objector would not exist — would thus be in a very poor position to present his objection!

With the Nicene Creed — confessed by all true Christians, whether Eastern Orthodox, Roman Catholic, or Protestant — I "believe in one God, the Father Almighty, Maker of heaven and earth, and of all things visible and invisible."

Why do I believe in this God of the historic church? Because, as St. Paul well put it, "The invisible things of Him from the creation of the world are clearly seen, being understood by the things that are made, even His eternal power and Godhead" (Rom 1:20). But the person of Jesus Christ is an even more powerful reason to back up the Psalmist's claim that it is "the fool" who "says in his heart, there is no God," for Jesus is simply inexplicable apart from the existence of the God He incarnated.

Granted, the church's statements about God are anthropomorphic; they could not be otherwise, since they are made by human beings, and since God entered the human sphere in Jesus Christ. But the issue is not whether they are anthropomorphic — the issue is whether they are *true*. One achieves exactly nothing (except perhaps ambiguity) by substituting phrases like Tillich's "Being itself" for the biblical descriptions of God. Indeed, as I have emphasized in my recent work, *The 'Is God Dead?' Controversy*, the obscurity and vagueness of much contemporary Protestant theology of the liberal variety has borne predictable fruit in the death-of-God movement. The God Hamilton and Altizer execute is the God of Tillich, Robinson, and Pike — not the God of biblical faith and historic Christian confession.

IV. PIKE

I affirm belief in God and in a personal God. I base this belief on two observable aspects of reality. First, that there is a universe. That is, that things do hang together and have unity to them. And second, that there is a certain measure of order and predictability on which science and technology rest. For example, there are repeatable items, instances of love, certain forms of recognizable beauty, etc.

Therefore, by faith, not by proof but a plausible inference from data, I affirm that there is a *unus* in the universe. I say *unus* rather than *unum* because also observable is human transcendence, those factors which distinguish people from things — self criticism, planning of life, tying together past, present, and future, the capacity to reveal oneself and receive the revelation of others, the capacity to articulate, etc. This has evolved in the universe. It is reasonable to suppose that it has been in the mix all along, since no stream rises higher than its source. *Nemo dat quod non habet.* Thus, that which we mean by human personality, "at least" that, would be attributed to God. At least, of course, is an important phrase . . . otherwise there would be an obvious anthropomorphism.

There are limits, however, as to what we can affirm of an element in reality, an *unus*, a ground of being, if we are to use modest inference from data. For example, I no longer affirm the customary *omni's*, such as omnipotence, omniscience, etc., since this would be an extrapolation way beyond any available observable experienced data. Also to affirm omnipotence, omniscience and omnibenevolence, raises a problem I cannot answer. That is the traditional problem of evil. In *A Time For Christian Candor*, I have a chapter on this subject, setting forth the six or seven customary answers to the problem and in all candor show that none of them pan out. In any case, it is not necessary to make these affirmations, since in terms of action and human relationship to God and human empowerment by God and our being channels of His truth-courage-love, our own blocks, idols, and hang-ups prevent the bonus of what we can affirm from manifesting itself (that is, in the case of most of us), and the lack of the ability to affirm more is, existentially speaking, not a serious problem, whatever it may mean intellectually. Here I would go along the line of Prof. Leslie Dewart in his *The Future of Belief* that while we cannot affirm the omnipotence of God, we can affirm the radical openness of history which not even the freedom of man can block.

Also there is something to be said for the "becoming" idea of God, if we are to be existential. As far as we can see, the increasing exercise of transcendence of man makes God more alive all the time, quite contrary to the death of God concept. Here Father Johannes Metz is illuminating in his reminding us that Yahweh means "I will be what I will be," and that we have to make true what we affirm, or rather we are in the process of making true what we affirm by way of doctrine and belief.

V. HAMILTON

The characteristic of radical theology, at least in the form that I am working on, is that it is trying to see if it is possible to think and live as a Christian without God. When we say God, we do not simply mean some inferior or naïve form, rather we mean the Christian doctrine or doctrines of

God of the classical mode. Now this means that some kind of god may be possible. It means that the theological function of renaming the gods in the time of the death of God may be taken on, and any God or gods that men may discover for themselves will be post-Christian and therefore non-Christian. Therefore, when Leslie Dewart or Eugene Fontinell defines God as the developmental or processive character of reality and consciousness, I would acknowledge that reality has this character, but to name this fact God seems impermissible for a Christian. As when Harvey Cox names "openness to the future" as God, I want to say yes, one ought to be open to the future, but I see no grounds for naming this posture God.

In other words, the radical who is trying to do his work without God claims there is a classical tradition in Christian thinking and it is that tradition to which he has to say "no." This means that he may need to find ways of doing in his own vision what God does in the classical vision, but it does not mean he brings in substitute forms of God. It means that Jesus without becoming divine takes over certain of the functions of God, and it means that the human community without being divinized or being idolized must take over other functions. The conservative wing of the radical theology is the most insistent that it must do its Christian thinking and believing and acting without the Christian God.

2. Jesus Christ

I. JONES

Jesus' identification as the Son of God is supported in Scripture by many incontrovertible testimonies. "Thou art the Christ, the Son of the living God," said Peter in answer to the Lord's question as to His identity (Mt 16:16). "This is my beloved Son, in whom I am well pleased," declared the Voice from Heaven at His baptism (Mt 3:17) and again at the Transfiguration (Mt 17:5). "Of a truth thou art the Son of God," confessed the disciples who saw Him still the troubled waves of a stormy sea (Mt 14:33). "That holy thing which shall be born of thee shall be called the Son of God," announced the angel Gabriel to Mary (Lk 1:35). "I saw, and bare record that this is the Son of God," testified John the Baptist (Jn 1:34). Many others — John the beloved disciple (Jn 3:16–18); a man born blind, whose sight was restored by a miracle of Jesus (Jn 9:35–38); Martha, in whose home He visited (Jn 11:27); Mark (1:1); and Paul the great Apostle (Acts 9:20) — also testified to His divine Sonship. Even the Powers of Darkness recognized and obeyed Him. Demons said to Him, "What have we to do with thee, Jesus, thou Son of God? Art thou come hither to torment us before the time?" (Mt 8:29). "The Father sent the Son to be the Savior of the world," wrote John (1 Jn 4:14, 15). "Whosoever shall confess that Jesus is the Son of God, God dwelleth in him, and he in God."

II. HENRY

In the flesh Jesus Christ is the incarnate Logos, the divinely promised Redeemer of fallen mankind, the supernaturally

14

born Savior who fulfills the Old Testament prophecies. He lived a life of perfect obedience to God in the flesh, thus demonstrating in human nature what true sonship to God implies, and by His sinless life and atoning death providing the substituted righteousness on the ground of which God alone spares the repentant sinner. His miraculous deeds were not simply works of power but signs of His redemptive mission and, above all, evidences of His divine Sonship. By His bodily resurrection He carried human nature forever into the presence of God. He bears the moral and spiritual image to which regenerate man is progressively conformed and to which the redeemed in the future resurrection will be fully conformed. In view of the progressive self-disclosure of God as triune, He is scripturally identifiable as the second person of the Godhead and the risen and exalted Lord of the Church.

III. MONTGOMERY

There is an old joke about an argument between a Jewish and a Roman Catholic boy. The Roman Catholic boy boasted that he could enter the priesthood — and some day might even become pope. When his Jewish friend was unimpressed, the Catholic boy said: "Well, what do you want? You want me to become Jesus Christ?" The Jewish boy replied smugly: "One of our fellows made it."

This is exactly what I *don't* believe about Jesus Christ: that He was just an ordinary person who climbed up to Godhead. Jesus was not the ideal boy scout who spent a three-year ministry helping little old ladies across the Sea of Galilee. He was absolutely unique, for He was no less than God in the flesh, come to earth to die for the sins of the world. "No man hath ascended up to heaven," He declared, "but He that came down from heaven, even the Son of man" (Jn 3:13).

As a matter of fact, if you or I claimed for ourselves the things Jesus claimed for Himself, we would be carted off for an intensive period of shock treatment. Said Jesus: "I and the Father are one, He who has seen Me has seen the Father"; etc., etc. He forgave sin (thus exercising a divine prerogative) and was ultimately crucified on the charge of blasphemy. To try to make Jesus into a humanistic ideal instead of a divine Savior is to run counter to all the historical facts about Him.

The Church — Protestant, Orthodox, and Catholic — always has confessed a Jesus who was "very God of very God" as well as true man. As C. S. Lewis nicely put it in *The Screwtape Letters*, any other "Jesus" is a product of demonic perversion, not historical fact: "The documents say what they say and cannot be added to; each new 'historical Jesus' therefore has to be got out of them by suppression at one point and exaggeration at another, and by that sort of guessing (*brilliant* is the adjective we [devils] teach humans to apply to it) on which no one would risk ten shillings in ordinary life, but which is enough to produce a crop of new Napoleons, new Shakespeares, and new Swifts, in every publisher's autumn list."

IV. PIKE

We do not know all human history and biography, nor do we know anything about conscious sentient beings on other planets. Hence, we must limit affirmations about the uniqueness of Jesus or the servant image of Jesus we see in the New Testament, which is the center of our focus in terms of that limited knowledge. On the other hand, one can affirm that, and I do affirm that, here is the best picture we have seen of the saying, the living out, the being a channel for the ultimate ground.

Jesus must be conceived of as a free man, capable of making decisions; otherwise we would have the monothelite heresy, the one-willism which would attribute only a divine will. Hence, I cannot affirm an incarnation that is "laid on," that is at birth, but rather follow the line of Luke 2:52, "Jesus grew in wisdom and stature and grew in favor with

4. The Virgin Birth of Jesus Christ

I. JONES

Had Jesus Christ been born with a human father as other men are born, He would have fallen heir to sin as, indeed, all generations since Adam and Eve have been children of sin — have had in their bodies the seed of sin. But though Jesus Christ was born of woman as other men are, His birth was supernatural also; for there was no earthly father. "The birth of Jesus Christ was on this wise: When as his mother Mary was espoused to Joseph, before they came together, she was found with child of the Holy Ghost." The angel of the Lord appeared unto Joseph in a dream, and said to him, "Fear not to take unto thee Mary thy wife: for that which is conceived in her is of the Holy Ghost. . . . Then Joseph . . . took unto him his wife: And knew her not till she had brought forth her firstborn son: and he called his name JESUS" (Mt 1:18–26).

"When the fulness of the time was come," says God's Word, "God sent forth his Son, made of a woman. . . ." (Gal 4:4, 5.) Christ's being born of a virgin is essential, or else God is a liar; and "God is not a man, that he should lie. . . ." (Num 23:19.) He is "a God of truth and without iniquity" (Deut 32:4). It is "impossible for God to lie" (Heb 6:18). If Jesus Christ is not virgin born, He fails to meet the conditions that God said His Son would meet as to the manner in which he should come into the world. The Virgin Birth is essential to the deity of Christ. Moreover, it is as much an essential part of salvation as is the death of Jesus Christ on the Cross.

Some men teach that it is possible to be a Christian without believing in the Virgin Birth. It is not. A man, when he comes to trust Christ as his personal Savior, may not know what the Bible says about the Virgin Birth; but when he trusts Christ, he will not doubt any miracle of the Word. Whoever questions the miracles of God's Word has not experienced the miracle of regeneration. Only the virgin-born Son of God has power by His death and resurrection to save sinners. He "was delivered for our offenses, and was raised again for our justification" (Rom 4:25). To disbelieve the Virgin Birth is to disbelieve the Christ who has power to forgive sins; for if He be not born of a virgin, His death has no value for the forgiveness of sin.

II. Henry

Jesus Christ was born of the virgin, Mary, by a miracle of the Holy Spirit. He entered history, as He left it, by a dramatic and decisive miracle. The virgin birth is explicitly affirmed by Matthew, a keeper of public records, and by Luke the physician, a scholar knowledgeable in medical science. Jesus' supernatural entry into the world is implied by John (1:14), if not explicitly taught (although in some early texts John 1:13 reads: "who was born not of blood, nor of the will of the flesh, nor of the will of man, but of God") and perhaps implied by Paul (Gal 4:4, 5). Since Luke was Paul's traveling companion, it is highly presumptuous to contend that Paul "knew nothing about a virgin birth." If the virgin birth were, as Helmut Thielicke contends, merely a metaphor expressing pious reflection on faith or, as Bultmann holds, a legendary expression for the dogma that the source of the meaning of Christ's person cannot be seen in His natural, earthly advent, and not as historical and theological fact, one cannot explain why this literary device does not recur throughout the New Testament. The virgin birth is connected with Christ's work of atonement — not as the only way in which God could have established the Son's uniqueness from the first, but as the way in which He chose to do so. The Messiah's virgin birth is foretold in Isaiah 7:14. The Apostles' Creed affirms the doctrine in juxtaposition with Jesus' sufferings under Pontius Pilate and bodily resurrection, indicating its literal assertion by early Christianity.

III. MONTGOMERY

The Virgin Birth occurred as a historical fact. It is recorded in the same primary-source records that tell us of Jesus' public ministry, death, and Resurrection. There is not one whit of textual evidence that the Virgin Birth accounts are "later additions" to the New Testament documents — all of which, in the judgment of the world's foremost biblical archeologist, W. F. Albright, were written "between the forties and the eighties of the first century A.D. (very probably sometime between about 50 and 75 A.D.)." If the old Fosdickian canard is raised that the Virgin Birth appears only in two Gospels (Matthew and Luke), then one need only recall that the Sermon on the Mount *likewise* appears only in those two Gospels — but few people try to argue that it is unhistorical!

Agreed that God could have come into the world in different ways. But this isn't the question. The question is: How *did* He come into the world? To answer such a question, we must go to the historical accounts and allow them to speak.

Of course, what really bugs certain theologians about the Virgin Birth is the miraculous character of it. But one must face the fact that historic, biblical Christianity is a religion centering on God's miraculous intervention in the world. This advent was predicted through miraculous prophecy, and attested to by the miraculous creation of the Church by the Holy Spirit on the day of Pentecost (cf. Charles Williams' *The Descent of the Dove*). And the earthly life of our Lord was miraculous in its substance and in its culmination (the Resurrection). Why then boggle at His miraculous birth?

And if miracles get on our nerves, then we have Newtonian not Einsteinian nerves. For us, living in the wake of Einstein's revolution in physics, the universe is no longer a tight, safe, predictable playing field in which we know all the rules. Since Einstein, no modern has had the right to rule out the possibility of events because of prior knowledge of "natural law." Ironically, the theological demythologizers (who claim to be eminently up-to-date) are nineteenth- or even eighteenth-century "modern," for they live and think in a world where the Virgin Birth and the resurrection can be rejected *a priori* — apart from any historical investigation. Such a view is hopelessly unempirical and unscientific — to say nothing of being impossibly untheological. The New Testament writers, who had personal contact with the miraculous events of Christ's life, were well aware of the distinction between myth and fact, and proclaimed the Virgin Birth as fully factual. "We," they write, "have not followed cunningly devised myths when we made known to you the power and coming of our Lord Jesus Christ, but were eyewitnesses of His majesty" (2 Pet 1:16).

IV. PIKE

I do not deny, since there is no empirical basis on which to deny, nor do I affirm the virgin birth. My difficulty is not the old-fashioned one of science and religion and miracle, etc. The freedom of science itself from the old-fashioned absolutes does not require one to reject the virgin birth, if there were firm data on which to affirm it. My difficulty lies rather in the fact that the New Testament data themselves would seem to point the other way. I summarize these data in a footnote in *What Is This Treasure?* In short, the Pauline writings do not mention it. If this had been part of the traditions at that time, it would be sufficiently important, or at least unusual, for him to have mentioned it at least *en passant*. In fact, he refers to Jesus as born of a woman under the law.

men were shepherds; some were scholars; some were peasants; and two of them were kings. Moses, the great Lawgiver, was brilliant; he was a graduate of the University of Heliopolis, and "was learned in all the wisdom of the Egyptians" (Acts 7:22). Other writers were "unlearned and ignorant men" (Acts 4:13). Naturally the style of these men would be different. God did not go beyond the style of each. Never did He force upon a writer some word not already in his vocabulary. Instead, out of each man's talent, experience, and vocabulary, God chose the right word and illustration so that His truth might be preserved in the writing. Any man who does not believe in verbal inspiration is in danger of not believing in inspiration at all.

II. HENRY

It would be folly to make claims for the Bible that it does not make for itself. Regarding inspiration, 2 Timothy 3:16 affirms: "All Scripture is inspired by God. . . ."

Regarding Scripture as God's Word, the Apostle Paul writes of the Old Testament as "the oracles of God"; and in 1 Thessalonians 2:13 he identifies apostolic proclamation "not as the word of man but as it is in truth, the word of God." And the Apostle Peter writes: "Not by will of man was prophecy brought at any time; but holy men of God spoke as they were moved by the Holy Spirit" (2 Pet 1:21). Addressing His contemporaries, Jesus Himself said: "Ye err, because you know neither the Scriptures nor the power of God" (Mt 22:29). If the Bible is the Word of God it is inerrant; what is errant obviously cannot be the Word of God. To say that the Holy Spirit or an authoritative Church somehow makes an errant Bible "the inerrant Word of God to me" simply obscures the transfer, in such theories, of infallibility from the Bible to some extraneous and superior principle, and subverts the doctrine of the objective authority of Scripture. Those who distinguish between portions of the Bible which are trustworthy, and portions which are fallible, never have agreed on any objective criterion whereby this distinction can be effectively applied. They simply substitute some external speculative demand or an act of will for the authority of the Bible.

The Bible is not a textbook on science and history; it is the divinely inspired book of redemption. But the divine plan of redemption is cosmic and historical, and revealed religion therefore demands a specific view of nature and history. Where Scripture explicitly teaches truth about history and nature it is wholly reliable. Christians ought not to demand a complete reconciliation of the scriptural revelation with the scientific and historical theories in any generation, since such theories are subject to refinement and revision; in the last analysis, the Bible judges them, not they the Bible.

In summary, the Bible is God's inspired and authoritative interpretation of sacred history, and the infallible revelation of His nature, deeds, and purposes. It is the authoritative rule of Christian faith and practice, and by it all other affirmations about supernatural realities are to be tested.

III. MONTGOMERY

Is the Bible inspired? In a word, Yes! With all the great theologians of the Church history, today's Christian ought to hold that Sacred Scripture stands above all criticism and proclaims an absolutely veracious message to all men.

Said St. Augustine: "In an authority so high, admit but one officious lie, and there will not remain a single passage of those apparently difficult to practice or to believe, which on the same most pernicious rule may not be explained as a lie uttered by the author willfully and to serve some higher end." Likewise Luther, with his characteristically no-nonsense declarations: "The Scriptures have never erred" and "It is impossible that Scripture should contradict itself; it only appears so to senseless and obstinate hypocrites." The *Westminster Confession of Faith* took the same stand: "The Supreme Judge, by whom all controversies of religion are to be determined, and all decrees of councils, opinions of ancient writers, doctrines of men, and private spirits, are to to be examined, and in whose sentence we are to rest, can be no other but the Holy Spirit speaking in the Scripture."

Why such a consistently strong biblical position on the part of Christendom's great theological spokesmen? Because the test of a great theologian is not his *originality*, but his *fidelity*, and the Augustines and Luthers of the Church have wanted to be entirely faithful to their Lord Christ in *His* approach to Scripture. When, at the beginning of Jesus' public ministry, the Devil quoted Scripture at Jesus in the wilderness, our Lord didn't say: "Oh, come now, we're too sophisticated for that sort of biblicism; let's get down to issues!" Rather, Christ did him one better — He quoted Scripture right back at the old evil foe, and capped it off with Deuteronomy 8:3: "Man shall not live by bread alone, but by *every word* that proceedeth out of the mouth of God." For Jesus, Scripture (the existing Old Testament and also the soon-to-be-written, apostolic New Testament — see Jn 14:26, and cf. 2 Pet 3:15–16) was totally and entirely God's word, and the Christian needs to view it in the same way. (And if he doesn't — if he criticizes it — he is really claiming to have a "revelation-to-the-second-power" which is capable of judging Scripture. But how could such a second-degree revelation be justified? And wouldn't *that* authority then require a revelation of the *third* power above *it*, and so on? here "Little bugs have littler bugs, and so *ad infinitum?*")

As for alleged contradictions and errors in the Bible, I like the observation of the Scandinavian theologian Valen-Sendstad: "It is remarkable that the nature of these so-called mistakes generally varies to correspond to the hearts and eyes that are contemplating them."

Moreover, the Bible is a clear and self-interpreting book, if we allow it to speak for itself. It requires no magisterium to tell us what it means, and, indeed, whenever a church or sect has set itself up as the authoritative interpreter of Scripture, the result invariably has been the obfuscation of God's word by fascinating but heretical human opinions. The story is told of a rather pompous cleric who gave his cleaning lady a big, fat, and learned commentary on the Gospel of John for Christmas. A month later he asked her if she was finding it useful. "Well, sir," she said, "at first I couldn't make head nor tail of it, but, you know, the Gospel of John has helped me greatly to understand it." Luther hit the theological nail nicely when he said: "The idea that in Scripture some things are recondite was spread by godless sophists who have never yet cited a single item to prove their crazy view; nor can they. And Satan has used these unsubstantial specters to scare men off reading the sacred text, and to destroy all sense of its value, so as to insure that his own brand of poisonous philosophy reigns supreme." Scripture, and Scripture alone, is the antidote to man's poisonous pastime of creating God in man's own image.

IV. PIKE

Here I would stand with Bishop Francis Simons, the Dutch Roman Catholic Bishop of Indore in India. In a footnote on the new morality in the Fall, 1966, issue of *Cross Currents*, he questions whether we can in any sense speak of the inspiration of Scriptures today. What is true in the Scriptures, or what seems to ring true, whether a matter of fact or principle or ethic or inspiration or insight, is made true by its correspondence to what would seem to be plausible inferences from experienced reality. Therefore, in the Scriptures we have quite a mixed bag of truth, of error, of sound ethics, unsound ethics, of myth in the best sense of the word, and legends — some useful, some apparently not so useful. The worldview of the time of writing and the public of the particular writer very much influenced what was said.

The books selected officially from a larger pool of books for the Old and New Testament by the Old and New Israel have a certain priority, and should be taken seriously because of the corporate approbation of them. Also these writings are

II. HENRY

At his creation man was neither a subhuman animal nor a morally neutral innocent, poised at the crossroads of amorality and morality. Rather, as Genesis affirms, he was fashioned in God's image, a rational, moral, and spiritual agent in active fellowship with God. To the first man God gave magnificent freedom in all areas but one: the determination of right and wrong, which He reserved for Himself. When Adam sought to usurp this moral authority, he fell. That this original sin had consequences not only for Adam but for the whole human race was a matter of divine decree. Each man might have been his own Adam before God, and found guilty on account of his own transgressions alone. But every man is condemned in Adam, and inherits the guilt, corruption, and penalty of his sin. Whoever protests that this involvement in the deeds of another is unjust also cuts himself off from the possibility of justification on the ground of Christ's righteousness. God in sovereign justice and grace has included in Adam all men who everywhere attest their inherent sinfulness, and He embraces in Jesus Christ all who trust the Righteous Substitute as their Redeemer.

III. MONTGOMERY

This venerable doctrine generally is misunderstood, and the reason lies, I think, in the word "original." It does not mean that man "invented" sin (he can't even claim that for himself — Satan beat him to it!). "Original" is what Oxford philosopher Ian Ramsey calls a "sacral qualifier" — a word that points up the full dimensions of a religious truth. Sin is "original" in its *extensivenes* and its *intensiveness*. With the exception of Christ, all human beings have violated God's perfect will and the dictates of their own consciences. This was true of the first man and his progeny (whether he had long arms and scratched himself or not) and will be equally true of the last man (whether he will have an enlarged noggin or not). "All have sinned," says Scripture, "and have fallen short of the glory of God" (Rom 3:23).

In Genesis we read of man's original fellowship with God and his subsequent alienation — through self-interest — from his Creator. The Hebrew word *Adam* means man-in-general. It is the equivalent of the Greek word that lies at the root of the English term anthropology. Anthropology is not the study just of Mr. A or Mr. B, but of man-in-general. Similarly, the Genesis account of the Fall deals not only with our first parents (and obviously we had some!), but also with all other men who have lived and who will ever live. "You should read the story of the Fall," said Luther, "as if it happened yesterday, and to you."

Original sin means, then, that we are all "east of Eden" (Steinbeck's novel nicely captures the essence of the biblical phrase). No one can sit in a house by the side of the road and watch the sinners go by. It is the fundamental pharisaic error to think that there is such a house. In point of fact, to use Beatnik poet Jack Kerouac's line, we are all "on the road," and the payment for that trip is established by a firm minimum-wage law: "the wage of sin is death" (Rom 6:23).

IV. PIKE

In the light of evolution and the likelihood of polygenesis, and in the light of the rather late origin of the Edenic myth, we can no longer sustain the historical basis of original sin, the fall of man, etc. The image found in Genesis does portray man's condition — it is in every man — "Adam" meaning a man. The various paradoxes in it are on the whole quite sound if given good exegesis, although sometimes you have to reach for it a bit. It does portray the sociological and psychological conditioning toward self-centeredness. The fact is that sin or virtue or right or wrong answers in regard to various ethical encounters are not simply a matter of a simple free will, yea or nay. We are caught up in a web of sin, as it were; man is born into a bent world and there is not as

II. HENRY

Man is not as bad as he can possibly be; in fact, the whole scheme of law and order is predicated on the assumption that he can and will respect civil law, and that if he does not he is subject to penalties. The fact that God wills the State, that even unregenerate men share in the promotion of humanitarian ideals, and that some become exemplary in their sacrifices for others, indicates that public justice and love of neighbor are not totally unattainable divine demands upon humanity. Human wickedness is not a mechanical necessity of human nature; it rather expresses man's explicit decision and moral revolt, for which he is accountable. Hence, in contrast with naturalistic evolutionary theories, revealed religion insists on the dignity of man — not indeed as a "higher animal," but as a qualitatively distinct creature, made for fellowship with God (and capable even now of restoration to that fellowship), offered the prospect of conformity to the holy image of Christ, and faced by destiny in eternity including resurrection of the body. He has, therefore, a possibility of regeneration that marks him off qualitatively from the animal world. Biblical Christianity pledges every repentant sinner what evolutionary naturalism simply cannot: final conformity to the image of Christ and a life fit for eternity.

But man is nonetheless corrupt — a fallen creature, in revolt against his Maker and prone to sacrifice the interests of others to his own. His corruption lies essentially in this: that he is by nature a sinner, that is, he does not love God, nor does he love his neighbor as himself. He may, and indeed does, do much that avoids the worst he might do; but even when he now does the best he can do, he acts out of inferior motivations and for ultimately selfish ends, rather than for the glory of God. And the verdict of historians on human culture leaves no doubt of its character; civilization after civilization has collapsed, and in modern times the worst world wars in the annals of man were provoked by two of the most literate and highly educated nations in history. Human civilization seems in our own time to be degenerating at a frightening pace. By these trends evangelical Christianity is confirmed in its conviction that only the scriptural regeneration of man can reverse or arrest the decline of human nature and history.

III. MONTGOMERY

Sin did not destroy human nature. If it had, then God could not have become man to save us from our sin, for God then would have had to become a sinner. Moreover, if sin were basic to human nature, then human beings could never enter heaven, for the removal of their sinfulness by Christ's work on the cross would be the removal of themselves!

Contemporary existentialist theologians, as well as those, like Tillich, who have been much influenced by existentialism, have gotten into this kind of pickle by asserting that man falls "from essence to existence" — that Creation and Fall are really coterminous and equally necessary to the definition of man.

Actually, sinfulness is not the product of man's nature; it is the result of man's freely chosen misuse of his nature. God created man with free will, with the high privilege of choosing to serve God or to serve himself. As C. S. Lewis so effectively argued, love cannot be forced, and it must always accept the possibility of rejection. God, who is love, gave His creatures the choice of loving Him or not, and they, in choosing to be free of God, fell into a bondage of the most absolute kind. Said Jesus: "Truly, truly, I say to you, every one who commits sin is a slave to sin" (Jn 8:33–34). This bondage so conditions each subsequent generation that the choices open to the children of sinners become sinful choices within an already sinful context — and the race wanders in a labyrinth that has (humanly speaking, in Sartre's words), "no exit." The children of Adam have the freedom to choose their own poison, but not to perform curative operations on themselves. Only the Great Physician — Jesus Christ, who "was in all points tempted like as we are, yet without sin" (Heb 4:15) — can provide the remedy we need, for only He did not succumb to the disease. And in not succumbing, He displays what human nature properly is, and shows men the noble potentiality which God can actualize when sin's drag-effect is removed.

IV. PIKE

The answer is both, and my answer here is somewhat a reflection of what I have said previously about Original Sin. There is present in the individual a capacity for good within or without religious traditions. Increasing good gets done in society, with increasing capacity to do good in a bigger and bigger way with the very rapid growth of science and technology and other areas of enlightenment. The capacity to do evil, to play out the full results of self-centered aims, also has increased with equal rapidity.

V. HAMILTON

The tragic, intractable character of human nature seems to me to be true and was appropriately rediscovered by American theology in the 30's and the 40's, given our experience of depression and war. Today we must build on the rediscovery of the tragic element of life. We must build on the so-called pessimism of the new orthodoxy revival and notice that life has another element too: men can in fact make decisions that count, and the newer technologies, far from being merely depersonalizing as traditional critics of technology like Erich Fromm and Herbert Marcuse and Paul Tillich have said, are in fact technologies that enable our decisions to count. Therefore there is a case not for the nobility of human nature, but for a more modest optimism about both personal and historical possibilities today.

8. Sin

I. JONES

The best definition of sin is that in Isaiah 53:6: "All we like sheep have gone astray; we have turned every one to his own way; and the Lord hath laid on him the iniquity of us all." Sin is rebellion against God. When Adam sinned, instead of meeting God in the cool of the day, he fled from God's presence to the deep shadows of the garden. Sin drives men from light to darkness. Because men are sinners, they "loved darkness rather than light" (Jn 3:19), and "in him is no darkness at all" (1 Jn 1:5). Sin manifests itself in many ways, but sin is a heart condition of rebellion against God. Sins are the fruit that grows on the tree of sin. It is because man is a sinner that he sins. Man does not become a liar because he lies. It is because he is a liar that he tells lies. "Out of the abundance of the heart the mouth speaketh" (Mt 12:34). A man does what he *does* because he is what he *is*. "For out of it" (the heart) "are the issues of life" (Prov 4:23). Social reform and reformation seek to shake off the fruit from the branches. Regeneration lays the axe to the tree. The sinner goes to hell not because God wants him to go to hell, for the Bible tells us that it is not the will of God that any should perish but that all should come to repentance (2 Pet 3:9). The sinner goes to hell because he will not do the will of God in coming to repentance and turning to Jesus Christ for salvation. Going into hell is the final act of rebellion on the part of a sinner who rejects God's love, spurns God's grace, and refuses God's Son.

II. HENRY

Sin is any want of conformity to the moral character of God and transgression of His revealed will. Essentially, it is failure to love God with one's whole being, and one's neighbor as oneself. Explicitly, it is the violation of God's revealed commands, the observance of which (in the spirit of love which Christ enjoined as the supreme commandment) is the outward evidence of one's love of God and gratitude for the redemption that is in Christ Jesus. Since the fall of man in Adam, man cannot do what he ought to do — and what he could have done, had he preserved his moral integrity; yet he knows that to disown the "moral ought" upon his life is destructive of his humanity. The predicament of man is not simply that he commits sins — as indeed he does, daily, in thought, word, and deed — but that he is a sinner by nature, and hence in need of a new nature or character. His will is bent against the commands of God and his mind is not stayed on his Maker; he displaces God at the center of his life and sets his affections on earthly things. He is self-seeking, and in all he does, even in his humanitarian efforts, he seeks to preserve above all his own security.

III. MONTGOMERY

Someone has defined sin as the thing that causes us to look up our own name in the telephone directory as soon as it is delivered. This is not too inaccurate (though one would hate to give the impression that only bourgeois westerners with telephones are sinners), for it points up the common element in all sinning: Self-centeredness and pride — the conviction that in the final analysis we are the center of the universe. Lucifer convinced himself that he was "like the most High" — and was "brought down to hell, to the sides of the pit." All sinful acts are attempts to set ourselves above God's will — to make ourselves "the master of our fate and the captain of our soul" — to engage in self-deification. The inevitable result is the destruction of a right relationship with God, and a corresponding fracture of human relationships on all levels — personal, national, and international.

In the nineteenth century, many persons came to look upon sin as nothing more than the unfortunate traces of earlier, less civilized stages of human existence. It was argued that man could move forward to idealistic perfection. Had not man improved greatly since the barbaric Middle Ages? Was not man making tremendous strides in science, medicine, and the arts? The early twentieth-century autosuggestionist Coué summed it up in a recommended adage: "Every day, in every way, I am becoming better and better."

But the wars, both hot and cold, of the last half century have shown that man, instead of becoming better, had only become more efficient. He had managed to arrive at the lofty pinnacle where he could kill and maim more of his fellow human beings in less time than ever before. True progress! Six million Jews and Hiroshima!

And if we are honest with ourselves, we will admit that these identical tendencies exist in us. You haven't killed? Anger toward a fellow man is made of the same stuff, according to Jesus. You haven't committed adultery? "I say to you that everyone who looks at a woman lustfully has already committed adultery with her in his heart" (Mt 5:27-28). Liberal and radical theologians of our day who are trying to revive nineteenth-century optimism about man are doomed to disappointment, and their naïveté is appalling. Such views are possible only in those too young (or too senile?) to remember Verdun or Dachau — or too insensitive to see the face staring back at them in their shaving mirror.

IV. PIKE

Sin is a possibility where freedom exists. We are not as free as we thought before the time of Freud, for example, taking into account compulsions and conditioning. At the same time, I do believe in a measure of human freedom and, therefore, sin is a reality. This is a wrong choice under the claim of responsible decision-making which is upon all of us. The claim is well stated in the Sh'ma Yisroel, "Hear O Israel, the Lord thy God is one Lord, thou shalt love the Lord thy God with thy whole heart, thy whole mind, whole soul." There is only one of Him and since He can claim all — there are no other gods and no other file of claims upon us. The codes of ethics are relative and historical analysis, historismus, in other words, show their changing character. They are not absolutes. They are guidelines and there can be no absolute answer to a given ethical question except in the context of the particular question. Even then our judgments are, of course, fallible. I accept the theory of situation ethics, approaches of situation ethics (sometimes called the new morality), as is shown in my revised edition of Doing The Truth, published in 1964 by Macmillan. A 1966 book of mine called You and the New Morality uses 74 cases to spell this out. It also is apparent in my book, Teenagers and Sex, published by Prentice Hall.

V. HAMILTON

In a technical sense, of course, the radical cannot even have a doctrine of sin, if sin is defined as coram Deo (a sin against God). But insofar as we have access to both the tradition and the documents I find myself going back to Genesis 3. I do not focus on the so-called act of disobedience or rebellion that Eve is supposed to have committed, which was the part of Genesis 3 that the classical Christian stressed. Rather, I would point to that part of the chapter where sin is seen as the violation of the human community, as that break in the human community in which Adam says to the Lord, "The woman whom thou gavest to be with me, she tempted me and I did eat," and the woman blames the serpent and thus the community of harmony between man, woman, and nature is

broken. It seems to me that here is a description of the consequences, at least, of sin. To overcome sin is therefore either
to heal our broken communities or to improvise new ones.
Politics as well as words of forgiveness seem to be a genuinely
Christian answer to sin.

9. Heaven and Hell

I. JONES

I believe in a literal Heaven and a literal hell. In the book of The Revelation, we have a full description of the heavenly city. I do not believe this can be spiritualized or held merely a symbol. The description is too accurate and the exact dimensions are given. But I believe there are many more wonders there than God describes, for He tells us it has not "entered into the heart of man, the things which God hath prepared for them that love him" (1 Cor 2:9). Nothing with which man is familiar in this world can be used to describe realities which exist in Heaven. They are beyond human comprehension or earthly comparisons.

By the same token, I believe that the picture of hell in the Bible is a literal picture — a place of eternal suffering. But I believe it may be infinitely worse than human language has power to describe or human thought to conceive.

The Bible warns us to "flee the wrath of God." It says that "it is a fearful thing to fall into the hands of the living God" (Heb 10:31). A sinner, guilty before God, should quake in his boots. America needs some strong preaching on hell such as that of Jonathan Edwards, who is said to have preached on hell with such force that people held onto the pews, for they could feel themselves falling into hell. Great revivals occurred under that type of preaching. Today, however, the trend is toward a sentimental, superficial emphasis upon "love," which is not scriptural. There is a dearth of good, sensible, hard-hitting biblical sermons on hell and the wrath and judgment of God.

II. HENRY

Heaven is wherever God manifests His essential glory. Throughout His creation God is everywhere present, not only in His activity but personally. But He specially manifests Himself in certain places and times. So His indwelling of believers distinguishes them from unregenerate men, and His incarnation in Christ distinguishes the Nazarene even from believers. In heaven — a realm of God's creation inaccessible to all who are under His wrath — He ultimately manifests Himself to creatures who bear His holy image and whose hearts are fixed on Him. Jesus Christ, who came from the Father's presence and returned thereto, knows more about fellowship with God in the invisible realm than any other man, and He explicitly said to His disciples: "I go to prepare a place for you" (Jn 14:3). Heaven, therefore, is not simply a spiritual condition, although it is at least that; Jesus promised to abide in the hearts of His followers before they are reunited with Him in the eternal abiding places (Jn 14:28; cf. v. 3). Heaven is God's "dwelling place" and, by His grace, the place where God fully indwells believers and they forever dwell with Him in holy joy.

Hell is a place of separation from God, reserved for those under divine condemnation. It also is a spiritual condition, now anticipated in the life of the unredeemed who are in a state of spiritual death. But Hell as a place is the abode of those who finish this life outside of Christ and under God's wrath. The physical death of the sinner marks the moment when his condition of spiritual death, which is reversible by repentance and faith in Christ, is transmuted into a condition of eternal death, which removes the impenitent forever from the possibilities of Heaven and seals his fate in Hell upon whose inhabitants the wrath of God abides.

III. MONTGOMERY

Heaven is a place most certainly, for, though "no man hath ascended up to heaven," Christ "came down from heaven"

(Jn 3:13) and told us that in His Father's house were many mansions. Indeed, Jesus said, "If it were not so, I would have told you" (Jn 14:2), the implication being that it should not even have been necessary to make the point with those who had committed their lives to Him. "The way ye know," continued Jesus: "I am the way, the truth, and the life; no man cometh unto the Father, but by Me." Heaven, then, is best characterized as the place where Jesus is. In a multi-dimensional universe such as ours, that "place" may be in our space-time continuum or it may not; perhaps, as a counter-world, it embraces our world at this very moment. We don't know; but we do know *that* it exists and that Christ has gone to "prepare a place" for those who trust Him with their eternal destiny.

Describing heaven is very dangerous business, and the lady-angels and harping saints of popular fancy frequently have resulted in a throwing out of the baby (the reality of heaven) with the bath water (the unbiblical mythology). In contrast to this sort of thing, I find especially helpful and eminently scriptural the late C. S. Lewis' stress on heaven in terms of *joy* and *depth*. In *Surprised by Joy*, his spiritual autobiography, Lewis described his lifelong search for something beyond mere happiness: joy, defined as an experience that one would want repeated forever. That is heaven — a condition (available in microcosm here and now) which, because Christ is at its heart, remains eternally fresh. In the last of his seven Narnia Chronicles, Lewis pictures the heavenly country as "world within world, like an onion: except that as you go in and in, each circle is larger than the last." In those circles, the children find the old mansion in which they first learned of the land of Narnia, for there "no good thing is destroyed." The new land was a "deeper country"; as one new inhabitant expressed it: "I have come home at last! This is my real country! I belong here. This is the land I have been looking for all my life, though I never knew it till now."

Hell is as real as heaven, for it is as clearly taught by Christ as is the reality of heaven. To pretend that hell doesn't exist or to rationalize it away accomplishes as little as putting one's head in the sand or ignoring the fact of cancer.

Heaven is where Christ is, where men and angels glorify Him and thereby become what they really are. Hell is where egocentrism reigns, and fallen men and angels destroy their personalities by endeavoring to exclude Christ in favor of themselves. "He that findeth his life shall lose it: and he that loseth his life for My sake shall find it" (Mt 10:39). The exclusion of Christ means the exclusion of all good, since He is the source of all good, so hell is a terrifying condition to contemplate. But it is a condition which one creates for himself as he chooses to live apart from Christ; and the man who insists on running his own life in this world will obtain that horrifying privilege in the next.

Wrote W. H. Auden of Christian littérateur Charles Williams: "The popular notion of hell is morally revolting and intellectually incredible because it is conceived of in terms of human criminal law, as a torture imposed upon the sinner against his will by an all-powerful God. Charles Williams succeeds, where even Dante, I think, fails, in showing us that nobody is ever *sent* to hell; he, or she, insists on going there." Williams' description of the damnation of a woman who insisted on being her own god captures the essence of biblical teaching on the subject and ought to give us all pause: "She cried out, 'You thought you'd got me, didn't you?' They saw the immortal fixity of her constricted face, gleeful in her supposed triumph, lunatic in her escape, as it had at once a subdued lunatic glee in its cruel indulgence; and then she broke through the window again and was gone into that other City, there to wait and wander and mutter till she found what companions she could."

IV. PIKE

As images for directions of life, heaven and hell are perhaps suitable. Obviously they are not locations, an impossible thought in a post-Copernican world view. I cannot conceive them as finalities. I believe in a personal conscious survival of the individual. I believe that there is growth (or its reverse, shriveling) of freedom and of openness through encounter, through significant moments or occasions when there is the chance for defensiveness or a "hang-up" to go or an idol to fall. I believe that this process goes on in life and here-after. I believe that in death we are where we are in this regard, and should hopefully grow from strength to strength, to quote the Book of Common Prayer, 1928. Some of those who die are more fully open to God — the case of Jesus is quite appropriate. We refer to his "glorious" resurrection. In the case of most of us, certainly myself, the phrase *comme çi comme ça* would certainly be more appropriate. I believe the after-life offers room for growth, chance for growth, further encounter, further relationships in which either open more widely and abandon something which has interfered with God's filling us and using us — or on the other hand, further close us in and lock us in.

A sorting of everybody out to heaven and hell would be a contradiction in terms because those who would be the type qualifying for heaven would not be in bliss knowing that a lot of other people were permanently and forever blocked from growth and were in torment. Also, if there is no freedom of movement or change in the life to come, then those in the life to come are not persons but things.

V. HAMILTON

On heaven, and hell and Satan, the radical cannot have anything to say. I don't want to say I reject or I don't believe, though that is of course, true. But there is a kind of stridency and arrogance in this kind of talk, and I don't see that there is any virtue in my having to say no. This is a kind of turning one's back on adequate and exciting conceptual equipment that does not seem to me to be useful, necessary, or possible today.

10. Satan

I. JONES

Satan, the Bible tells us, was a covering cherub, a creature of light, who because of his pride and rebellion was cast out of heaven together with the angels who followed him. Satan, the devil, is not in hell. He is "the prince of the power of the air." He is not omnipresent, but he is the commander of a vast host of evil spirits. As the ruler of the world society, he offered to give our Lord the kingdoms. He was tempting our Lord to take a shortcut. It is the will of the Father that Jesus Christ shall have the kingdoms of the world, but God willed that He reach the Throne by way of the Cross. Had Satan succeeded in bringing Christ to bow the knee to him, then Satan would have succeeded in setting himself above God — in bringing God into subjection to him. Satan opposes all those who seek to do the will of God. He endeavors to hinder the preaching of the Gospel; he inspires the persecution of Christians; he delights in human suffering and iniquity of all sorts. But the Word of God tells us that some day he will be cast into the lake of fire.

II. HENRY

Jesus Christ knew more about the nature of the invisible moral order than any other man. He not only represented Satan as a personal agent and source of evil, but depicted His own redemptive ministry as centering in the overthrow of Satan's dominion. It is impossible to reduce these affirmations to an accommodation to Jewish ideas of his own age. When the prevalent theology collided with spiritual truth, Jesus did not hesitate to condemn it. Moreover, if He accommodated Himself here, by what criterion (other than the divergent speculations of modern thinkers) is a line to be drawn between His teaching and such concessions? Further, if Jesus wrongly connected evil with a personal Satan, why is it so surely asserted (by those who argue thus) that Jesus rightly connected good with a personal God? Why not go the whole distance with naturalism and consider the Nazarene as mistaken here also, or as given to accommodation?

Satan is a creature of the angelic world whose revolt against the Creator antedates the fall of Adam, and whose strategy is to coordinate all the forces of evil against the will of God. His power was broken by the triumph of Jesus Christ over death, sin, hell, and Satan himself. His power over believers is greatly curtailed by the indwelling Holy Spirit, and his prospect is final doom.

III. MONTGOMERY

The great American evangelist Dwight Moody was once asked why he believed that the Devil existed. He answered: "For two reasons. First, because the Bible says so. Second, because I've done business with him." Moody was right on both counts. In fact, twentieth-century man has done so much business with Satan that not a few people (for example, some students I knew well at Cornell in my undergraduate days) find it easier to believe in the Devil than in God!

C. S. Lewis astutely wrote in the preface to his *Screwtape Letters*: "There are two equal and opposite errors into which our race can fall about the devils. One is to disbelieve in their existence. The other is to believe, and to feel an excessive and unhealthy interest in them. They themselves are equally pleased by both errors and hail a materialist or a magician with the same delight."

As the Church fathers recognized, however, Satan — who can never create, only pervert — frequently overplays his hand through pride. The great *fin-de-siècle* French novelist J.-K. Huysmans so involved himself in satanic and occult activities that finally they convinced him of the reality not only of supernatural evil but also of supernatural good; after returning to the Church shortly before his death he wrote: "With his hooked paw, the Devil drew me toward God." Christianity is not a dualistic religion (like Zoroastrianism, for example) in which Satan exists on an equal plane with God; in the final analysis the Devil is, to use Luther's phrase, "God's Devil," and even his machinations are used against him in the councils of eternity.

IV. PIKE

I do not believe in Satan in a literal sense or even in a meaningful symbolic sense. The demonic, as a category of the structures of evil that are larger than the individual, is a useful category. Angelology and demonology seem to have been much underlined through the Zoroastrian influence, particularly intense in the Essene sect (as the Qumran Scrolls show), and on into the New Testament and Christian tradition.

V. HAMILTON

See comment under "Heaven and Hell."

11. What Must a Man Do to Be Saved?

I. Jones

A man is saved by "grace through faith." This is "not of works" (Eph 2:9). Baptism has no part in salvation. Neither do good deeds nor charity. Our salvation depends upon the work of Christ on the cross. The Bible says, "The plowing of the wicked is sin" (Prov 21:4). In other words, even the legitimate labor of a sinner is sin because he is a sinner. He has received no spiritual life from God. He does not take God into account, and he is dead unto God. It is no more possible for an unsaved person to do a work of righteousness than it is for a corpse to do a day's work in the field or factory.

Those who emphasize the life and teaching of Jesus and neglect the blood of Jesus Christ are lost. The only hope for a sinner is the fact that God loves him and gave His Son; that the Son laid down His life as ransom for many — that He paid sin's penalty by dying on the Cross to save man from sin; and that faith in Him brings life — eternal life. "The blood of Jesus Christ his Son cleanseth us from all sin" (1 Jn 1:7). There is no other cleansing. If Jesus Christ had not died, there would be no hope for any sinner. Had He come merely to teach men and nothing else, we would have new condemnation heaped upon us, for nobody would be able to live up to His teachings. The law condemns us because we are unable to keep it. It is "our schoolmaster to bring us unto Christ, that we might be justified by faith" (Gal 3:24).

II. HENRY

To please God, one must love God with his whole being — and this includes fulfilling all God's commands. Had Adam lived in obedient love of God, he would not have fallen. If there is salvation for the ruined sinner — and, thanks be to God, there is — it can be only because a gracious God so wills, and He alone stipulates the conditions. Since man's works no longer can save him, but rather condemn him, and the holy Creator dignifies righteousness even in His manifestation of grace, He promises redemption by faith in the righteous Substitute. Jesus Christ is the Redeemer who fulfills the Old Testament figures, promises and prophecies; on the ground of His active and passive obedience — that is, of His sinless life and atoning and reconciling death — we are offered the forgiveness of sins and new spiritual life. To be saved (from sin and its consequences) man must personally acknowledge his need of salvation as a sinner and "believe in the Lord Jesus Christ" (Acts 16:31). Salvation is therefore a gift — "not of works lest any man should boast" (Eph 2:8).

But the reason the sinner turns to Christ is to escape sin and its consequences. Hence one who truly accepts Christ no more allows sin to dominate his life, but submits it to Christ's lordship (Rom 6:12 ff.). Good works are not the ground of salvation, but supply evidence of salvation (Jas 2:14). What God has in view in the redemptive rescue of sinners is their restoration to fellowship with the Creator of life and to holiness.

III. MONTGOMERY

Scene: The Admissions Desk, Heaven. *Characters:* St. Peter and Mr. Religious (a pillar of community and church for many years).

St. P: To enter here you must have earned 1000 points.

Mr. R: That doesn't seem excessive. I was a community

leader for thirty years and strove for better government and general social improvement.

St. P: Excellent! A praiseworthy record. That's one point.

Mr. R (taken aback): I was a faithful family man — married to the same woman forty years and the father of three fine children whom we sent to the best schools . . .

St. P: You don't say? We don't get many like you these days. That's another point.

Mr. R (sweating freely by now): I was a scout leader, attended church every Sunday, was a member of the church board, taught Sunday School . . .

St. P: Commendable in every way! What a credit you were to the community. Two points. Now let's see, that makes . . .

Mr. R (on his knees, almost prostrate, half mumbling to himself): Good Lord! But for the grace of God, nobody could get in here!

St. P: You have just received 1000 points.

To be saved, a man must first recognize that he can't save himself. Why? Because everyone has willfully violated God's perfect standards, and he who "offends in one point of the law is guilty of all" (Jas 2:10). God's standard is perfection, as Jesus said in the Sermon on the Mount, and this means we all desperately need divine grace. To enter a ball park when the admission price is $1 is just as impossible if you have 50¢ as it is if you have only 10¢. People who say, "All I want on the Day of Judgment is what I deserve" will get exactly that — to their horror.

God's grace is given freely in Christ, who died for our sins on the cross. This grace comes to us through the Word (the Bible) and the sacraments or ordinances (Baptism and the Lord's Supper), and we appropriate it through faith. This is the great truth of "justification by grace through faith" that the Reformers proclaimed on the basis of Scripture itself: "By grace you have been saved through faith; and this is not your own doing, it is the gift of God — not because of works, lest any man should boast" (Eph 2:8–9).

Faith, moreover, is not "the magic of believing" (as a book title has it). It is not faith-in-ourselves, or faith-in-faith. It is faith in *Christ* — the faith that cries: "God, be merciful to me a sinner." This never is mere intellectual assent. In the original Greek text of the New Testament "believe in Christ" literally means, "believe into Christ" — "enter into a living, personal relationship of trust with Him." The saved man is the man who (in Augustine's words) accepts God in Christ as the center and circumference of his life.

IV. PIKE

Man is in the process of being saved, that is being made whole, through responding positively to encounters, through not clutching at the idols, and being open to change. Thus the divine Reality can operate through him and cleanse him and make him fruitful and effective, loving, creative, etc.

V. HAMILTON

Is Christianity a religion of salvation at all? Can salvation be separated from its gnostic, supernatural and other-worldly dualistic elements? Bonhoeffer, at the end of his prison letters, denied that Christianity is a religion of salvation. But let's assume that "salvation" is the word we choose to use to describe what the Christian thing gives: a certain quality of life. "Repent and believe," is the traditional language in answer to this question, and I do not see any difficulty with this if the word salvation is to be retained. "Repent" means to make a decisive and visible alteration in the self-centered character of one's life, to recognize that man is fulfilled only in community, only in relationship to his neighbor. If man is to enter into the Christian thing, be saved in this sense, not in the other worldly sense but simply to be located in the Christian community, he must in some sense say yes. This is the "believe" part of repent and believe. Man must come to believe Jesus, as the one to whom he owes a discipleship.

12. Divorce and Remarriage

I. JONES

The Lord answers quite clearly the question of divorce and remarriage in Matthew 19:6, when He states, "What therefore God hath joined together, let not man put asunder." Certainly no pastor should be a divorced man, because the scriptural standard is that the Bishop should be "the husband of one wife" (1 Tim 3:2). (I believe the celibacy of the Catholic clergy is condemned here.)

II. HENRY

Monogamous marriage is biblically enjoined, and husband and wife are bound to each other until death dissolves the marital partnership (Rom 7:1 ff.). Since sexual intercourse is part of the marital due (1 Cor 7:3–5), the marriage contract is not considered binding where it is not or cannot be thus consummated. Celibacy may be preferred for one's larger freedom in the service of Christ, but it is not required of all ministers of Christ, nor is it a sign of superiority of person or office. Marriage is desirable and normative. Where one partner forsakes the other, remarriage by the offending partner frees the other from the marriage contract. Prior to remarriage by the deserter, the forsaken partner faces serious questions of conscience: whether the deserting partner can still be reached for Christ, and the home reconstituted. Freedom to remarry is not, therefore, the only consideration. But fornication, or adultery, by either party, is ground for divorce (Mt 19:9). Yet the emphasis of the New Testament falls on the power of love to heal sin.

III. MONTGOMERY

Jesus admitted only one valid ground for divorce — adultery (Mt 5:32 — and there is not one whit of textual evidence that this passage has been doctored, pace the liberals). Malicious desertion is not a *ground* for divorce, it *is* divorce, so remarriage is legitimate for the deserted partner in such cases (1 Cor 7:15). But even in these sad cases, the ideal is to win the erring partner back, for a married couple are "no more two, but one flesh; what therefore God hath joined together, let not man put asunder" (Mt 19:3–6). As for the "burnt toast" variety of grounds for divorce permitted in some states and by some clergymen, Jesus would have had none of it.

On the other hand, it is important to note that the scriptural standards in these matters are set for *believers*. Because of the "hardness of hearts" Moses allowed a less strict divorce procedure and this received qualified approval from Jesus (Mt 19:7–9). Thus Christians ought to recognize that for unbelievers divorce and remarriage on non-biblical grounds may sometimes be the lesser of evils. But an evil it is, and it must not be rationalized as a good. The parties involved should be brought to see that such situations reflect our sinfulness and ought to drive us to the cross for God's forgiveness.

IV. PIKE

This is covered in my text on ethics, *Doing the Truth*, and in *A Time for Christian Candor*, Appendix A, with special reference to our own Church. An existential decision is involved here, a fallible one to be sure. In some cases, divorce is better than the continuation of marriage. If there is no way of restoring a given marriage, then, following the line of the "spiritual death" theory (as in the Orthodox Church from the time of early Eastern Christianity) a marriage can die as can persons, and remarriage could be a right decision in a given context.

V. HAMILTON

Divorce and remarriage seem to me to be human and social problems on which the theologian can claim no special expertise. I see nothing in the Christian faith that makes an effective case against divorce as an unfortunate but genuinely human necessity.

13. Pre-Marital Sex

I. JONES

I do not know any born-again, Bible-believing minister who would not condemn pre-marital sexual intercourse or any other kind of immorality. The Christian standard is cleanness of life. God's blessing is upon sex in marriage. The Bible emphasizes the sanctity of the home and purity of heart and of thought. The so-called "New Morality" is immorality. Man's attitude toward God's standards may change, but the standards are as unchanging as the God who set them and "whatsoever a man soweth, that shall he also reap" (Gal 6:7).

Every Christian church or educational institution should stress the fact that pre-marital chastity is essential to a young person's Christian victory. In the forty years since Bob Jones University was founded, no unmarried co-ed has gone home pregnant and in disgrace. Out of the hundreds of marriages made on this campus during those years, less than a dozen have ended in the divorce courts.

II. HENRY

Pre-marital sex (in the contemporary understanding, intercourse) is sinful. The "new morality," which deplores a principle ethic, hoping thereby to intensify existential involvement in moral decision, issues instead in unprincipled immorality. Some of its champions, who say that pre-marital intercourse cannot be said always to be wrong under the same circumstances, but that it is wrong 98 percent of the time, offer no objective basis that precludes inverting the statistics and justifying immorality in most cases. What they offer is not an authentic biblical morality, but a neo-ecclesiastical version that simply stays one step behind the concessive secular mood, and dignifies this with a Christian label.

It is tragic that sex in relation to Christianity suffers violence at the hands of both Roman Catholic and liberal Protestant traditions, the latter in relation to pre-matrimony, the former in relation to matrimony (in the insistence on a celibate clergy and the exclusion of the marital use of contraceptives on the basis simply of a good conscience toward God).

III. Montgomery

In the little town in New York State where I grew up, there was one church that totally condemned dancing and most other forms of social contact between young people. The church was quite successful in this, except for one little difficulty: there were far and away more illegitimate births in that congregation than in any other church in the community! Why? (a) The pastor was so busy preaching against things the Bible leaves as open questions that his preachments against true immorality were lost in the shuffle. (b) The young people had nothing else to do. I look on that church situation as parabolic. If "pre-marital sex" means normal social contact between the sexes, then the Christian faith wholeheartedly approves. The kind of sex shibboleths characteristic of Bob Jones University are not only unbiblical; they are plain crazy and produce just the opposite effect from that described.

But if pre-marital sex means intercourse before marriage, Christianity says No! unqualifiedly (the biblical word "fornication" refers in part to such activity). Situation sex is utterly un-Christian, for it violates the high analogy drawn in Scripture between Christ and the Church on the one hand and the faithful husband and wife on the other (Eph 5:22–32). To have intimate relations outside of marriage is the equivalent on the human level of idolatry on the spiritual level (1 Cor 6:13–20). When Bishop Pike, in such writings as his *Teen-Agers and Sex* (1965), gives existentially-oriented parents guidance in counseling teen-agers in the use of contraceptives and countenances abortion for pregnant teen-agers under certain "psychological circumstances," he prostitutes (and I use the word literally) his ministerial office.

IV. PIKE

I know of no absolute basis for saying no in this regard. In weighing out a given decision in context there is much more to take into account than sometimes is taken into account. For example, as in the *Playboy* philosophy or recreational view of sex, I would readily grant that sex is recreation, a good thing in itself, fun, etc. But it also is sacramental in character, an outward and visible sign of the invisible spiritual grace or union. It both symbolizes and expresses this relationship and it is a means of grace. Unfortunately, often in sex there can be imparity in emotional involvement. This imparity in involvement can cause serious harm even though each party clearly understood at the beginning that less than full commitment was involved.

All these factors sound orthodox enough, so that I sound like "no" on the subject when I write on it and speak on it. However, I ground it on a contextual or situation basis, not an ontological or natural law or authority basis. Here I refer to *Teenagers and Sex* and *Doing the Truth* and *You and the New Morality*.

Should there be a "yes" given in the context, right or wrong, then further responsibility exists in regard to what used to be the three blocks or arguments against pre-marital sex, but which now can be handled, namely, conception, infection, and detection. There are still responsibilities there whether or not the initial decision was a sound one.

V. HAMILTON

I have been on the sex circuit for some time and I'm one of the few theologians of the non-conservative kind that has published defenses of pre-marital chastity as a legitimate option. I do not think there is any line of inference to be drawn from a biblical or Christian word to pre-marital chastity. I do think of pre-marital chastity as simply one of the possible choices the young man and the young woman can make as a way of handling their sex life today. I think, as a matter of fact, it is the only way in which the body can be taken seriously and that sex can be affirmed.

This comes from a conviction that sex is good not only instrumentally but symbolically. I do not defend pre-marital chastity as a dogma that Christians have to line up behind, but simply try to make a case for it so that a minority of young people today can have a good conscience about making this choice. A good deal of the sexual crisis is based on conformism in which one assumes that pre-marital sexual experimentation somehow is necessary. I'm against any kind of conformism. If chastity can be defended on the grounds that it is an eccentric moral option that one or two people ought to hold today, then it should be used.

14. Racial Integration

I. Jones

Certain standards of separation are clearly set forth in the Word of God. Paul, preaching at Mars Hill, reminded his hearers that men are all made of one blood; but he does not stop there. He continues, "and [God] hath determined the times before appointed, and the bounds of their habitation" (Acts 17:26). And Paul tells us *why* God fixes these boundaries — "That they should seek the Lord, if haply they might feel after him, and find him" (Acts 17:27). In other words, the divisions and the boundaries are there for man's spiritual good.

Fallen man has been trying to break down God's boundaries and build One World ever since the Tower of Babel. Man is attempting to achieve without the reign of Jesus Christ what God intends shall come only to the Glory of His Son. The cry today is, "One World, One Race, One Church"; but it will be a corrupt and evil world, a mongrel race, and the church of Antichrist. Intermarriage of the races is a breakdown of the lines of separation which God has set up and, therefore, is rebellion against God.

II. Henry

Race prejudice is a sin. The biblical doctrines of creation and redemption stress the equality of all men in the sight of God, and one's race ought to be a matter of indifference before the law and in the Church. There are, of course, cultural differences which have always accounted for voluntary preferences in association, and such liberty should be preserved where it does not rest on race prejudice or perpetuate injustice. It is not the task of the institutional Church to prescribe or promote specific legislative bills, but it is the duty of the Church to preach the whole counsel of God, to rebuke race prejudice, and to renew men in personal devotion to the will of God. Individual Christians should be in the vanguard of those seeking good laws, and supporting them. But the experiential answer to racial bias will await the shaping of new attitudes, reconciliation between men, and a sense of common humanity facing the abiding concerns of life. The religion of the New Testament, with its emphasis on the need of personal regeneration, and of the moral example of Jesus, holds promise of the moral dynamic to shape a new and better day. The answer to the race problem, therefore, will come at the deepest level when it is stated not in terms of black-and-white, but in terms of the problem of the human race before God.

III. MONTGOMERY

Racial integration is thoroughly Christian, for God created all men and Christ died for all men. The consequence is that "there is neither Jew nor Greek: ye are all one in Christ Jesus" (Gal 3:28). One of the greatest blots on the history of American churches is their toleration of the prejudicial treatment of minority races. No legitimate effort should be spared to help Negroes and other minorities to achieve full civil and social rights — and this requires direct opposition to unjust and immoral legislation (which, as a matter of fact, is not genuine legislation at all when it stands in opposition to God's eternal law!). "But, Dr. Montgomery, would you want your daughter to marry one of them?" "In a word, Yes! Better that my daughter should marry a believing Negro than a bigoted White who has forgotten the love of Christ and 'passed by on the other side.' "

IV. PIKE

We are not to treat persons as things. We do that when we use them. We also do it when we make pre-fab categories about persons and decide for them in terms of categories other than their own individual merit and capacity or opportunity for development. Therefore, any form of racial discrimination is wrong.

V. HAMILTON

I share the widespread feeling that the civil rights movement is breaking down. Integration as a short-range goal has broken down, and I agree with the kind of attack on integration as the ideology of the moderate that the early Stokley Carmichael and James Baldwin have often made, "Do I want to be integrated into a burning house?" In the time of the breakdown of the structures of integration, the black power movement must be taken very seriously. My objection to integration is from the left and not from the right. Ultimately it seems to me that America has to learn what it means to live in genuinely pluralistic society. This means a religiously as well as racially integrated community. But in the meantime, integration has been taken over as the ideology of a too slow, too moderate, and too complacent center in American racial thought today.

15. Anti-Semitism

I. JONES

Neither the Vatican Council nor anything else can alter the facts of history or change the truths set forth in the Word of God. At the trial of Christ before Pilate, the leaders of the Jewish nation cried, "His blood be on us, and on our children" (Mt 27:25); and it has been. But the Scripture makes it plain that, as a nation, Israel will be restored to her land and the Throne of David will be re-established with the coming of the Lord Jesus Christ to reign on earth.

Jesus Christ, after the flesh, was a member of the Jewish race — the seed of David (Rom 1:3), a child of Abraham (Heb 2:16). He fulfilled the divine promise to the patriarch, "In thee shall all families of the earth be blessed" (Gen 12:3). I cannot understand how a Christian could be caught up in the anti-Semitism that prevails in so many places. Born-again Christians ought to love the Jew, for out of this race came our Savior. Something is wrong with the Christian experience of one who does not have in his heart some love for these chosen ones of God and does not desire their salvation. On Israel now is a curse which dates back to the time when they rejected their Messiah. No race ever has been so persecuted and mistreated. The great proof of the Bible, somebody has said, is the fact that the Jews still exist as a separate race. They have lived in all the nations of the earth — have been captive in all kingdoms — yet their identity is still apparent. Wonderful race! As Jonah in the body of the whale was not digested, so in the sea of nations the Jews have not been absorbed. God has preserved them, and they have been a blessing wherever they have lived. The nations that have turned against the Jews have gone down. In the 15th century, about the time that Columbus discovered America, Spain turned against the Jews; and she, who once was possibly the most prosperous nation of Europe, now is the most wretched country in Western Europe. Miserable, dirty, depraved, backward, all her glory is departed. Hitler's notorious crimes against the Jews and the judgment that followed are well-known. The divine promise to Abraham, "I will bless them that bless thee, and curse him that curseth thee" (Gen 12:3) still holds. Believers are commanded to pray for the peace of Jerusalem. There is blessing for those who do.

II. HENRY

When one reads the Acts of the Apostles, with its setting in the aftermath of the crucifixion of Jesus, the Jewish attempt to stifle Christianity sets the stage for early Christian history. Yet the later persecution of the Jews by institutionalized medieval Christianity introduced a dimension of hatred into Christian-Jewish relations that staggers the imagination. The recent modern Nazi slaughter of six million Jews was, of course, instigated by a pagan ideology, though Hitler himself had a Roman Catholic background and Germany ostensibly was a Protestant nation. In the Middle Ages, the Jews were despised on the theory that all were directly guilty in the crucifixion of Christ; in the Nazi era on the theory that they are an inferior race. A Christian bound by the Bible can accept neither view, nor can he in any event despise the Jews of whom came Jesus of Nazareth according to the flesh. The Apostle Paul, himself a Jew, and an arch-persecutor of the early Christians, as a disciple of Christ could wish himself condemned that he might win some of his kinsmen to faith, and emphasized that the Jew has a continuing place in the plan of God (Rom 9–11). It is now recognized even in Israel that the Protestant Reformation is one of a chain of historical events that made possible the subsequent emergence of Israel as a nation. A new era of Christian-Jewish understanding is now happily emerging. The Vatican Council has removed offensive passages from its liturgy; Christians in America are more interested in the problems facing Jewish minorities, and in the new state of Israel more attention is being given to fulfillment of religious freedom, despite Orthodox pressure repressing Christian minorities.

III. MONTGOMERY

Anti-Semitism, and any other evil you can name, probably can be found in the life of some professing Christians. Why? I was recently reading an article by a scientist-who-is-a-Christian (one must watch the terminology here!), and he answered the parallel question, Why are so few scientists Christians? as follows: "For the same reason so few garbage collectors are Christian: *Sin.*" No one, except Christ, is perfect; Scripture declares: "If we say that we have no sin, we deceive ourselves" (1 Jn 1:8–10). But the Christian revelation, and Christ Himself, give no grounds whatever for justifying anti-Semitism. Indeed, in one sense Scripture holds the Jew *above* the Gentile: because God's Word came through the Jewish nation, the "gospel of Christ is the power of God unto salvation to everyone that believeth, to the Jew first, and also to the Greek" (Rom 1:16, etc.). The unbelieving Jew today is a man caught in a kind of time-trap (to use science-fiction terminology); he is living in an unrealistic past, as if the Messiah had not come and the Dayspring had not dawned on high. The gentile Christian, recognizing that he himself is but a "grafted-in branch" on the tree of salvation, will try in love to point his Jewish neighbor to Jesus, who is at the the same time the Jews' own Messiah and the Savior of all those who believe.

IV. PIKE

Anti-semitism is present to some extent among Christians. I refer to Glock and Stark, *Christian Beliefs and Anti-Semitism*, the best statistical study in this area. Part of this Anti-semitism is due to an erroneous way of stating the doctrine of the Atonement, and the Vatican Council did something very positive in this regard as have other churches such as the Episcopal Church at its 1964 St. Louis Convention. Part of it is a form of xenophobia, a fear of the unfamiliar, dislike of strangers. Anti-semitism, of course, is a great block in the Christian development historically. I feel greater progress is being made in this regard with the improving of Christian educational materials in the churches and greater care of what things are said from the pulpit and in Christian publications. Of increasing value are positive efforts for closer relationships with Judaism: theological dialog, common social action, greater personal relationship.

V. HAMILTON

Anti-semitism as a Christian phenomenon certainly is with us. I think that as Hitler and the death camps and the whole meaning of the holocaust emerges out of the unconscious into our consciousness today, that the indigenous anti-semitism of historic Christianity has to be faced far more radically than, say a Reinhold Niebuhr does, who thinks the problem can be solved by simply saying no to conversion of the Jews. There is a new dialog between the Jew and the Christian today that is attempting to move beyond brotherhood, into an actual theological dialog. This is quite different from the old dialog in which Abraham Heschel and Martin Buber were every Christian's favorite Jewish thinkers. This is quite different from the old dialog in which every Christian was an expert on what a Jew was and every Jew was an expert on what a Christian was. Wherever Christianity leads to anti-semitism we ought to be very clear in noticing that it may come from our beliefs and not just from our practices. Distinctions between belief and practice seem to me here to be very unwise indeed.

16. The Ecumenical Movement

I. JONES

The ecumenical movement is an attempt to build an ecclesiastical organization without a Scriptural foundation. In the Bible, the Church is the Body of Believers. The *ecclesia* is composed of the "called-out" ones — those who have been born of the Spirit of God through faith in Jesus Christ. They are "out of every kindred, and tongue, and people, and nation" (Rev 5:9). An ecclesiastical organization, whether it calls itself Lutheran, Roman Catholic, Methodist, or Baptist, is not *the* Church of the Scriptures. The ecumenical movement is building a unity of apostate ecclesiastical organizations. The "World Church" will be a larger ecclesiastical organization headed up by apostates — often blasphemous, frequently unclean and evil men — false teachers for whom is reserved the mist of darkness for ever (2 Pet 2:17).

We are living today in the Laodicean age of the Church which God is spewing out of His mouth, but He says that "if any man hear my voice, and open the door, I will come in to him" (Rev 3:20). The scriptural witness and testimony of Christ today is being preserved in individual local churches that will not bow the knee to Baal and in the lives of individual Christians who seek to obey God and who separate themselves from the apostolate ecumenical church.

II. HENRY

In its beginning the modern ecumenical movement was a cooperative effort of evangelical Protestants to advance common missionary and evangelistic concerns.

In this sense it remains a desirable trans-denominational objective. Evangelical Christians today would welcome a renewal of Christendom that would overcome not only Protestant proliferation, but the long-standing Roman Catholic-Eastern Orthodox fissure, if a new and deeper reformation once again would re-establish Christianity on a New Testament basis.

But any such expectation from the contemporary ecumenical movement is now unrealistic, for ecumenism itself has undergone a shift of outlook and goals in the twentieth century. The dominance of modernism over Protestant institutional structures in the early twentieth century refashioned the ecumenical ideal on the basis of a pluralistic theology — not on the basis of all Christians who subscribe to the ancient ecumenical creeds, but inclusive of neo-Protestants who renounce both cardinal doctrines of the Protestant Reformation and of the ancient creeds. Despite its affirmation of Jesus Christ as "God and Savior," the World Council of Churches, which now integrates Protestant and Orthodox churches into a neo-Protestant inclusive ecumenism, in practice compromises evangelical theology as the normative base of ecumenical unity. Despite the large number of evangelical Christians — Dr. John A. Mackay estimates that 25% to 33% of the conciliar affiliation is conservative evangelical — they are not given visibility in ecumenical planning or participation even on a par with deviant and maverick minority points of view. This accounts for the growing clamor among evangelicals both inside and outside the neo-Protestant ecumenical movement for a distinctive world church that would unite the many diverse and broken evangelical efforts into a cooperative trans-denominational body predicated on evangelical beliefs. Some influential leaders have discouraged such a move, on the ground that neo-Protestant ecumenism first should be given a full and final opportunity to reflect its intentions and practices in respect to evangelical Christianity, and that only then should a decision be reached on the issue of evangelical ecumenism. The post-evangelical temper of the Federal Council of Churches, of which the National Council is the successor, gave rise to the American Council of Christian Churches and the National Association of Evangelicals, and the latter body especially today represents a formidable body of Protestant Christians outside the conciliar movement. But in recent years the trans-denominational cooperation on an evangelical base has drawn the increasing interest of evangelicals inside and outside the conciliar movement yet hitherto unassociated with N.A.E. In England there has been growing demand for a national evangelical church. The relation of evangelical Christians to conciliar ecumenism undoubtedly will come to definitive determination within the next decade, and the answer will largely turn upon the principles and practices of the National Council of Churches and the World Council of Churches.

In respect to Roman Catholicism, evangelical Christians contend that virtually all the issues raised by the Protestant Reformation remain lively centers of concern. They welcome the emerging signs of religious tolerance, the larger interest in the Bible, and the new opportunities for dialog that have been shaped by the Vatican Council, although very few leaders in the evangelical movement were invited to Rome. Catholic observers were invited to the recent evangelical World Congress on Evangelism and, while commending its evangelistic concern, criticized its disengagement from the question of ecclesiastical community and structural organization.

III. MONTGOMERY

True, spiritual ecumenicity already exists among all Christians on the basis of their common relationship to the Lord of the Church, Jesus Christ. Organizational *union* (as compared with this already existing *unity*) is fervently to be wished for (compare Jesus' prayer, "that they all may be one"), but it must be pursued along proper lines. Union of churches is God-honoring only if it reflects agreement as to the contents of Christian truth. Mere emotional desire for a common Church ("ecclesiastical snuggling up") is not enough, and God's pure Word all too frequently has been obscured or lost in church unions producing more heat than light. (I like the comment about one big church that was created through ecumenical union of a lowest-common-denominator variety: "It's the church for those who don't care much for religion.")

Moreover, we Americans especially have to watch ourselves so that we don't bring into church life our favorite fallacy that "quantity makes quality." It is sobering to note that the modern ecumenical movement in the States gained its real momentum during the age of "big business" early in this century. Maybe the time has come for some anti-trust laws against church organizations. It is just possible that gigantic churches can become as impersonal, inefficient, and productive of "organization-man" attitudes as any cartel. Frankly, I don't think that Parkinson's law ought to replace either the law of Moses or Christ's law of love. The way to true ecumenicity is to draw closer to Christ; in Him unimportant differences melt away and love for His truth becomes all-consuming.

IV. PIKE

I've been very much involved in the ecumenical movement and have been the host of Dr. Eugene Carson Blake in proposing the Blake plan, which later became the basis for the Consultation on Church Unity. I do not believe that there are any essential differences in the teachings of the principal churches (I couldn't speak for every single sect); but members of various churches do feel that some of the things that I would regard as earthen vessels are, in fact, part of the treasure. Greater dialog brings out the fact that some of our difficulties are semantic. Some are due to differences of conceptual structure and some are due to exalting certain customs, mores, ways of thought, and traditions, into finalities. I think with the decline of Christianity institutionally throughout the world, there are practical reasons for unity which should push us farther along faster.

V. HAMILTON

To the ecumenical movement, every Christian to the left of right says yes. I say yes to it with some boredom because it seems to me in its present form to be theologically dull. As a theologian I have not looked to the ecumenical movement for any serious or constructive theology for 15 to 20 years. There was a time when the forward edge of theology was in the ecumenical movement. But today it seems to me to represent largely the theology of the safe center. However, I must acknowledge there are some very interesting things being done under ecumenical auspices. I'm thinking largely of the work of the youth committee in Geneva, engaged in an exciting work on the renewal of the Church and youth evangelism.

The ecumenical movement says that denominationalism is a sin, and I agree. To commit one's self to this idea is to commit one's self to a good thing, but we must initiate a far graver and far more serious dialog than the ecumenical movement has yet dared. The dialog between unbelief and belief is more basic than the dialog between Jew, Protestant, and Catholic, and until the ecumenical movement can genuinely constitute this, the unbelief-belief dialog will have to go on outside the ecumenical movement.

17. Liberal Protestantism

I. JONES

"Liberal" Protestantism (and I think the word "liberal" always should be written (with quotes) is neither "liberal" nor Protestant. The most bitter, uncharitable, and illiberal men are those who set themselves against the Word of God and who cannot tolerate opposition.

II. HENRY

Religious liberalism is a post-scientific secular view that left its mark upon all branches of Christendom, but only in Protestantism did it come to dominate and characterize major church institutions as a formative and decisive influence. Its confidence in the scientific approach to reality and truth led in turn to exaggeration of divine immanence, replacement of the Bible doctrine of creation by an evolutionary theory of origins, and unbelief in miraculous supernaturalism (e.g., the virgin birth, propitiatory atonement, bodily resurrection, physical ascension, and second coming of Christ). For the biblical emphasis on the sinfulness of man and the declension of history it substituted the notions of man's inherent goodness and inevitable progress borrowed from evolutionary speculation. Its link to Christianity was the emphasis no longer on the Christ of the New Testament but nonetheless on "Jesus as Savior and Lord" in the sense that the Founder of the Christian religion could — if men would follow His example of complete dependence on God — rescue them from inner personality conflict, and integrate their discordant selves into a harmonious existence — *better than* any other religious figure. Thus Jesus, while not held to be qualitatively distinct from other men, was held to be superior in degree of sonship to God.

Religious humanism struck at the insistence of liberalism on a special significance for Jesus, pointing out that the scientific method — which liberals had made their controlling principle in repudiating the miraculous — cannot support any such dogmatic claim. As humanists say it, *whatever* delivers man from personality discord and harmoniously integrates the self (an objective in which readers will recognize a grossly secularized version of the New Testament demand for the regeneration of the individual person) is to be esteemed as divine — whether as ideal person, cause, or movement. Thus the "new birth" becomes commitment to pacifism, civil rights, or some other ideal or person demanding total dedication.

Evangelical Christianity struck at liberalism from the other side, that of its obvious discontinuity with New Testament Christianity. Today liberalism has become less a fixed theological position (its doctrines are legion) and mainly a philosophy of social involvement and political engagement promotive of specific legislation; this philosophy looks largely in a socialist direction.

It is increasingly the tendency to emphasize the divergent schools of thought in Protestantism today. This diversity is sometimes stressed by (1) Catholic scholars emphasizing, by contrast, the doctrinal uniformity of the Roman Church; (2) secular scholars emphasizing the pluralistic character of American religion; (3) evangelical scholars protesting the inclusive nature of Protestant ecumenism.

It cannot be disputed that neo-Protestantism has become a pantheon of religions, for its theological spectrum ranges from fundamentalism to demise-of-God secularism, and many denominations have lost a sense of indignation in the presence of heresy. But evangelical Christians consider this a grievous miscarriage of the Protestant legacy and of apostolic Christianity. They protest, moreover, that the ecumenical dignifying of theological novelties gives them a prominence out of all proportion to their influence and importance. The great bulk of Protestant church members do not traffic in these deviant views. And in the case of the Church of Rome, which unquestionably has a monolithic character, there are significent major divergences, as between Thomists and Scotists, perpetuated by the various ecclesiastical orders, as well as concessions to modernism and existentialism by Roman Catholic scholars, of which the general public often is unaware. The problem of theological plurality today confronts all the major branches of Christendom. But it is especially critical in the case of Protestant Christianity.

III. Montgomery

Protestant liberalism is the bane of theological existence, for it commits the worst sin of all: it stands in judgment on God's Word instead of letting God's Word proclaim judgment and grace to it. It creates God in the image of man's own rational faculties or subjective interests, rather than letting God create us in the image of His Son. To become truly liberal — truly free — one needs to be freed from sin and error by Christ; but this is exactly what the self-styled liberal refuses, in the interests of his supposed intellectual or moral autonomy. Like Marlowe's Faust, he becomes a law unto himself; and Scripture, not without reason, calls Antichrist "the Lawless One" (2 Th 2:8). The first step in salvation is to stop talking back and listen while God's Word does the speaking. Would that liberals learn this simple truth before they, in full clerical dress, cut off completely the limb they are sitting on, and fall ignominiously to earth, to the glee of the unbelieving world (a posture well illustrated by the ministerial anti-hero of Peter De Vries' novel, *The Mackerel Plaza*).

IV. PIKE

I have difficulty with liberal Protestantism as a phrase. I don't recognize the existence of anything called Protestantism in reality. I think all churches should be Protestant in the Tillichian sense. Paul Tillich enunciated as the Protestant principle the fact that the churches are under judgment, needing reformation, or *semper reformanda*, a phrase being used in the Roman Catholic Church. But, if something is true, it's true. If it's Christian, it's Christian. I think all reformers have intended to state in a better way, a fresher way, or a truer way, or more original way, in the sense of being true to the early message, "What is the Christian faith?"

I suppose within the context I am a liberal Protestant, quite liberal, if liberal means open and not bound by finalities. Liberal Protestantism is a movement that was followed by neo-orthodoxy, but I think there is evidence now of a new form of liberal Protestantism very much on the scene. It bears many of the same marks and says many of the same things that liberal Roman Catholic writers and thinkers do. No longer is denomination the main distinction in regard to the range of theological opinions. Some Roman Catholic writers are to the theological left of many who might call themselves liberal Protestants.

V. HAMILTON

I have no special comments to make about this because I have never been a liberal or fundamentalist. Liberal Protestantism seems to me to have made a great contribution historically to the thought of the Church in that it has dared to say yes to the historical method, and we cannot go back on that. On the constructive side of theological options, liberal Protestantism seems to me to be an historic movement of no special interest today.

18. Fundamentalist Protestantism

I. JONES

May I begin by pointing out two things: First, fundamental Christians (that is, strong, Bible-believing Christians) generally are against smoking, drinking, dancing, card-playing, etc. But it should be borne in mind that their separation is not so much a separation *from* worldly practices as a separation *unto* the Gospel. They are not "fundamentalists" because they are *against* certain practices; but because they *are* fundamental in their theology, they refrain from certain things which they believe are condemned by the Scripture (either specifically or in principle) or which they believe will dishonor God and cloud their Christian witness and testimony.

Second, many of the various Pentecostal groups, which are often considered to be in the Fundamentalist circle are becoming ecumenically minded and are taking a very weak position when it comes to condemning apostasy. They are extremely active in Dr. Billy Graham's ecumenical evangelism, and many of them are affiliated with the National Association of Evangelicals. While they, therefore, would claim to believe the Bible and to be fundamental in their doctrine, they are not strongly scriptural in their practices concerning matters of ecclesiastical separation.

II. HENRY

Fundamentalist Protestantism would, I believe, subscribe to all the positive affirmations made previously. The classic

volumes titled *The Fundamentals* included essays by scholars
in mainstream churches who supported miraculous biblical
theism against the onslaughts of modernism. From this point
of view it is arbitrary to contrast fundamentalist and evangelical, and one may justifiably protest the assimilation of the
former term to fanatical extremists and the contrast of fundamentalism with neo-evangelicalism as if the latter were a
mid-twentieth century cult. Both champion the fundamentals
of the Christian faith.

Yet fundamentalism as a movement arose as a late nineteenth-century protest against liberalism. It concentrated attention on the "five points" that swiftly unmasked the
ambiguity of liberal preaching: the virgin birth of Christ as
opposed to merely supernatural origin; His deity (versus His
divinity as the latter term was being used), His substitutionary
atonement (not simply vicarious sonship), His bodily resurrection (in contrast to spiritual immortality), and His second
coming (as opposed simply to emphasis on the final triumph
of righteousness). This doctrinal program was summed up by
emphasis on the inspiration and inerrancy of Scripture, in
view of the higher critical tendency to honor Scripture only
when independently verified.

Thus fundamentalism marked two significant changes. It
emphasized doctrines selected for a polemical purpose against
liberalism, neglecting a full-orbed biblical theology. And it
made biblical inerrancy a hallmark, whereas not all evangelicals, although insisting that the Bible is infallible in
matters of theology and ethics ("faith and morals"), were
ready to espouse inerrancy in all scientific and historical
statements.

The World Christian Fundamentals Association, formed
shortly after World War I, incorporated belief in the pre-
millennial return of Christ and opposition to organic evolution to the fundamentalist stance (emphases over which
earlier contributors to *The Fundamentals* such as James Orr
would have balked). Subsequently, the fundamentalist movement was largely oriented to the dispensational teaching of

the *Scofield Reference Bible*, and the recent book *Neo-evangelicalism* by Dr. Robert Lightner of Dallas Theological Seminary draws a sharp line between dispensational premillennialists (as genuine fundamentalists) and "neo-evangelicals." Their tendency now is to categorize as neo-evangelicals those conservatives who have doubts about the inerrancy of Scripture beyond matters of faith and morals, and who are open to theistic evolution.

More recent developments disclose deep temperamental and emotional differences between evangelicals and fundamentalists. Almost all serious theology in the past generation has been contributed by the former, largely because of the preoccupation with polemics characteristic of the latter. The anti-communist, anti-ecumenical, anti-neo-evangelical, and in fact anti-National Association of Evangelicals crusade of Dr. Carl McIntire of the American Council of Christian Churches has further stamped one wing of fundamentalists as negative, reactionary, and isolationist. The distinctive assumptions of McIntire's program are that everyone is apostate who is identified with a church in the conciliar movement, and that the conciliar movement is irremediably oriented to un-Christian objectives. Similar premises underlie the attacks on the evangelistic ministry of Dr. Billy Graham by critics like Dr. Bob Jones, Sr., who contend that cooperative sponsorship of Graham's crusades by churchmen inside as well as outside the conciliar movement constitutes a worse danger to the Christian cause than liberals who openly deplore the Gospel. Both McIntire and Jones were highly critical of the 1966 World Congress on Evangelism in Berlin, which attracted evangelical delegates from 76 churches or denominations in 100 nations.

In summary, fundamentalism now is rapidly becoming that wing of the evangelical church which resists even evangelical ecumenism, is polemical rather than theological in orientation, and is divisive rather than cooperative in emphasis.

III. MONTGOMERY

While the liberal Protestant busily develops new forms of heresy, and forgets the eternal gospel of man's salvation in the midst of lady bountiful acts of charity, the fundamentalist manages to become totally irrelevant, so that nobody (except an already committed fundamentalist) listens to his (basically sound) proclamation. The central doctrines preached by the fundamentalist actually are the historic doctrines of the faith — as expressed in the Apostles' Creed. But the fundamentalist, fearful of the demands of modern life and unwilling or unable to meet the challenges posed by intellectual unbelief, retreats into a shell of blue laws ("don't go to the movies," "don't play cards," etc. — ad nauseam). Though many of these negative social rulings had some legitimacy in an earlier day (card playing, for example, was associated with saloons and prostitution on the American frontier of the nineteenth century), they function today as a device to wall off the fundamentalist from "the world" — which is seen as the Devil's playground instead of as the sphere of God's creative action. Thus the fundamentalist avoids the live issues of the day; and, ironically, like the liberal he opposes, he obscures the gospel by elevating man-made values to the level of divine truth. My Rx for both fundamentalists and liberals: Acquire a sense of history and of the Church's historic confessions; this will preserve you from absurd innovation (liberalism) and equally absurd reaction (fundamentalism).

IV. PIKE

Fundamental Protestantism is an extreme case of archaism. It gives a finality to everything in the Bible. It is difficult to know how they work out the inconsistencies. Take the New Testament, for example. Its authority rests on the Church-fact, on the bishops of the Church. It was they who decided which books belonged in the New Testament, and which "false claimants" should be rejected. Yet the Protestant Fundamentalist position is anti-episcopal, not apt to regard bishops as infallible. In other words, on what basis would they establish the authority of the scriptures absolutely? Sometimes they quote a passage from 1 Timothy which says all scripture is inspired of God. When you ask them what is their authority for accepting that as final, they say that since it is in the Bible, it is inspired. It is a kind of circular reasoning.

Further, on what basis would fundamentalists decide how many books belong in the Bible. Churches have differed on that — and still do today.

V. HAMILTON

Fundamentalist Protestantism seems to me to be very likely to increase in strength as it becomes more sophisticated. One of the interesting things about fundamentalist Protestantism is that it is proving to be a shrewd critic of mediating solutions to theological problems. They've tended to criticize Karl Barth. More recently fundamentalist Protestantism has pointed to the radical or "death of God" theology as showing that as soon as you leave the dogma of inspiration in any sense at all, this is the ultimate end. In many ways, I think the fundamentalists are right in saying there is no theologically stable position between themselves and the radical movement — though perhaps Roman Catholicism is an authentic alternative.

19. The Roman Catholic Church

I. JONES

I believe the Roman Catholic Church is described in the seventeenth chapter of the book of The Revelation, where she is depicted as the "great whore that sitteth upon many waters: With whom the kings of the earth have committed fornication" (17:1, 2). She is also "drunken with the blood of the saints, and with the blood of the martyrs of Jesus" (Rev 17:6). In the symbolism of the book of The Revelation, the waters are the peoples of the earth. The Roman Catholic Church has spread her power over the nations. She has aligned herself, wherever possible, with the civil powers and has used them to her own ends. She is clothed in the purple and the scarlet of the cardinals and the bishops. But her destruction is clearly prophesied and is as sure as the eternal Word of God.

There are many fine, sincere people in Romanism, and some of God's redeemed children are there just as some saved men and women are in apostate Protestant denominations; but God warns them to come out before this judgment falls.

The Bible prophesies the coming of a great "World Church" resulting from the union of all these apostate ecclesiastical organizations — "denominations," if you prefer that term — under papal rule. This "World Church" will serve Antichrist.

The papal claim to infallibility, blasphemous and arrogant as it is, is an essential factor in this coming religious union. There must be some sort of religious authority and, if the authority and infallibility of the Bible are denied, ecclesiasticism must look to a man as its source.

II. HENRY

Evangelicals respect the Roman Catholic Church as the largest of the three divisions of Christendom, but they reject its claim to be the only Church founded by Christ on earth and, moreover, share the verdict of the Protestant Reformation upon its religious institutions of the papacy and the sacraments as a departure from New Testament religion. Since the Council of Trent (1563) aligned itself against evangelical Protestantism, and evangelical missions have felt the brunt of religious intolerance in Catholic countries, both traditions have viewed each other as rivals. The view that the authority of the Roman Catholic Church — not the letter of Scripture — is the proximate rule of faith, has not been altered by that Church's encouragement of the laity's larger use of the Bible, and the approved translations still include the Old Testament apocryphal books as assertedly having the same divine authority as Holy Writ. Evangelicals welcome Roman Catholic assurances of a new attitude toward the "separated brethren" [even if non-committal about the ecclesiological validity of separated churches], and hope that long-standing restrictions in Portugal, Colombia, Spain, and Italy soon will be transcended. They also welcome new opportunity for dialog, perhaps even more fully at the level of neighbor relations with Catholics than at the level of official institutional engagement (partly because of discouragement over recent conciliar ecumenical trends). At the popular doctrinal level the chief evangelical objections to Roman Catholicism are its doctrines of the papacy, the immaculate conception, physical assumption and co-mediatorial role of the Virgin, and the failure to affirm justification by faith alone.

Most evangelicals, contrary to liberal Protestants, therefore are disinterested in active pursuit of merger with the Roman Catholic Church. They now often distinguish — although

Fundamentalists do not — between the Pope, who as a person may be devout, and the office, which seems to them one of gradiose ecclesiastical pretension. They do not consider it their duty to hurl every possible invective at the papacy, and are not bound by Luther's identification of the Pope as antichrist. But neither are they inclined — contrary to Greek Orthodox leaders — to accept the doctrine of papacy if the Pope can be regarded as "first among equals" whose significance is valid only for Roman Catholics. They recall that Luther's excommunication was approved by the Pope, and now that Rome is radically altering its view of Luther, they wonder whether a radical alteration of its view of the papacy is not also overdue. For evangelical Christians share Luther's conviction — with which the Church of Rome has not really come to terms — that the entire system of Christian belief is to be derived not from the Fathers and the councils but from the Bible, and that the task of councils is to defend the clear fundamental doctrines of Scripture.

III. MONTGOMERY

I cannot accept the so-called "Petrine theory": the theory that the true Church is that body maintaining a *successio personarum* (succession of persons) back to Peter as the first pope. For me, as for the Reformers, the only true succession is a *successio doctrinae* (succession of doctrine) which is determined by fidelity to Holy Scripture. Therefore I cannot accept the claims of the Roman Church, and I agree with Luther that, insofar as she proclaims that salvation involves man's cooperation with God (which is the exact opposite of the biblical teaching that salvation is by grace alone, as we have seen), she functions in the manner of an antichrist.

However, in practice, Roman Catholics in great numbers through the centuries have relied solely on the Christ of Scripture for salvation, and with the twentieth-century biblical revival in the Roman Church (stemming from the work of Père Lagrange and the École Biblique, etc.), more and more

Catholics are bringing their religious life into line with the scriptural Word. (This does not, however, gloss over the sad biblical liberalism manifested by some "New Shape" Roman Catholic theologians, such as Jesuit John L. McKenzie.) Today Protestant liberalism and theological radicalism pose a far greater threat to historic Christian truth than does Rome. If I were forced to choose between them, I'd see my travel agent for a ticket to the Eternal City tomorrow.

IV. PIKE

The liberal creative reforming edge of the Roman Catholic Church is the most exciting thing on the Christian scene, providing more inspiration, more life, more encouragement than anything else that is going. There is a large drag, a cultural lag, if you wish, in this regard as we know. In fact, outright tension and argumentation are going on. There is much tendency to reinterpret certain doctrines to make them no longer barriers. For instance, the Assumption of Mary into heaven is being defined by one or two prominent Catholic theologians as merely the selection of the leading saint to illustrate what is true of all of us, namely, ongoing life after death.

Infallibility, which seemed such a barrier, had some modification in the Vatican Council's position on the episcopate as collegiality. But in practice it is fading. I doubt very much if the Pope will on his own be pronouncing doctrines again. There is an authority crisis in the Church, noticeable particularly in the last few months where the various cautions and positions taken by the Pope are openly criticized and analyzed by liberal Roman Catholic journals and even rather conservative Roman Catholic journals. It would seem that it is no longer being assumed that what the Pope says is true just because he said it. Instead, the papal statements are being judged by the intellectual Catholic community by their own norms. There is an existential change occurring here, though not actually a doctrinal change in explicit terms.

I'm suggesting that there is more ground for hope for removal of the barriers between Roman Catholicism and other forms of Christianity. Changes are bringing us all closer, and dialog is showing this to be the case. This is much to be desired.

One wonderful thing about the Roman Catholic Church is that it at least knows that it is in a reformation whereas some of the other churches don't. Some Protestants think they already have had all the Reformation needed, and therefore there is lacking that fresh openness to hearing all views which I find in speaking at Roman Catholic institutions and talking to Roman Catholic theologians. This is not entirely a black and white matter, of course. There is much openness everywhere now but it has a naïve, fresh character in the Roman Catholic Church. This is due to the fact that it is a new experience for Catholics as compared to what has been true in non-Roman Catholic bodies.

V. HAMILTON

Aggiornamento and renewal of the Roman Catholic Church today can come only with great delight to anyone who sees the genuine liberation that one's Catholic friends are in the process of experiencing. I find many theological as well as ethical movements in the Catholic left today most exciting. Particularly in the work of Leslie Dewart and Eugene Fontinell in North America, I find a theological move partly parallel to the kind of radical theology that we're trying to work on within Protestantism. One of the most interesting theological experiences I've had was an all night teach-in that I shared with Richard Rubenstein of Pittsburgh and Eugene Fontinell of Queen's College at the University of Rochester in 1966. Here, without compromising the radical differences among us, one saw three men working very close to the same position, each in his own way, and all of them quite clear that they were faithful members of their own tradition. None were anxious to be well-thought-of by the other, none were sentimental about the differences, although differences were there, and indeed they became wider as we moved on.

The radical movement within Roman Catholicism I find exciting both theologically and in terms of the leadership Catholics are giving in politics and race and peace today. I find this whole ferment to be deeply moving. Whether it can be carried off as an intellectual and ethical movement with the aegis of Roman Catholicism is not something on which I can be certain. No more am I sure whether radical Protestant theology can be carried on within the structure of Protestant Christianity. I defined radical theology at the beginning as an experiment, and I would still do this.

20. Communism

I. JONES

Communism is a Satanic force. It is from the Eastern Communist bloc that the armies will come up against Jerusalem in an effort to destroy God's people Israel "that dwell safely" in the land (Ezek 38:11). A free nation, a democracy, either must oppose Communism or be destroyed by it. We should clean out the Communist sympathizers in our government and remove the men who are "soft" toward Communism, some of whom seem even to have come to cabinet rank. Private ownership of property is approved in Scripture. One of the situations that will exist under the millennial reign of Christ is that every man shall sit under his vine and his fig tree, and no man shall make him afraid (Micah 4:4).

II. HENRY

Communism is a totalitarian philosophy predicated on dialectical materialism, and it has gained world dominance to an extent unapproached by any previous totalitarian power in the history of man. It is an atheistic philosophy, explicitly anti-christ in that it ranges itself against the creation-redemption orders of history postulated by biblical revelation, in the interest of secular totalitarian revolution. But it is not the decisive enemy of the Gospel, despite the tendency of extremists to concentrate upon it as if it were the final incarnation of the demonic; if Christianity were not opposed by communism, it surely would be opposed by some other ism. Yet the fact remains that wherever communism is entrenched Christianity is disadvantaged, and in the long run they may be right who insist that either Christianity will regenerate the communists or the Free World defeat them on the one hand, or communism will destroy Christianity on the other.

Communism views the state as sovereign, and hence as the source and stipulator of all "rights." It proclaims a coming world revolution, including the elimination of private property, and advances its goals by force and violence wherever possible. It exploits the pockets of discontent and poverty in order to undermine every rival theory of life.

The survival of social injustice in areas where adherents of supernatural theism could do much to overcome it as a majority of the population provides communism with a propaganda opportunity to promote, at one and the same time, desirable social reforms, arbitrary social changes, and an atheistic theory of life. In this situation Christianity reacts naïvely when its leaders transform the institutional Church into an agency of direct political pressure and engagement in quest of material betterment. What is needed is the careful ideological definition of the will of God for man and society, the compelling support of supernatural theism over atheistic and materialistic views of life, the connection of a good conscience and good works with the profession of faith in Christ, a new emphasis on the public responsibility of Christians, and an evangelistic confrontation of the communist world.

III. MONTGOMERY

Christianity puts an imprimatur on no economic or political system. Neither capitalism nor communism, neither oligarchy nor democracy is "God's system." We do the gospel a great disservice when we uncritically identify it with "the stars and stripes forever" — with our "American way of life."

"Communism" (communal ownership of wealth) is thus not to be condemned per se by Christianity. But atheism is,

and so is totalitarianism (the subjugation of all life and values
to the state). Insofar as Russian or Chinese communism is
atheistic and totalitarian, *to that extent and for those reasons*
it must be rejected as demonic. But *if* (and it is a big if, ad-
mittedly) the Russian state continues to exert less and less
totalitarian pressure on its people, and *if* Marxist theoreticians
like Garaudy were to succeed in convincing the party that
atheism is not a necessary base for communist ideology, then
Christians would have no legitimate *theological* ground for
blasting Russian communism. Hochhuth's play *The Deputy*
(whatever we may think of its portrait of Pius XII), points
up the terrible danger of viewing communism as the worst
of all evils, thereby allowing the end to justify the means
in opposing it — with the result that even greater evils are
perpetrated.

Furthermore, there is something more than a little dis-
quieting in Jesus' teachings about not picking out specks in
other people's eyes before extracting beams from one's own.
Why, therefore, don't we American Christians devote some
time to cleaning up our own capitalistic mess, where self-
centered management tries to run roughshod over government
(remember the issue of steel prices?), where self-centered
and corrupt labor leaders try to make everyone knuckle-under,
even in time of war (Jimmie Hoffa inevitably comes to mind),
and where all of us in a fat-cat economy justify our fat cathood
in terms of individual initiative, while much of the world's
population goes to bed hungry.

IV. PIKE

Apart from the Chinese, there is a demythologizing going
on among the communists which makes possible Christian-
communist dialog, the type which had its grounding in the
Vatican Council and *Pacem in Terris*. I have had some involvement in this myself; others have done more, like Leslie
Dewart and Harvey Cox. We must realize that the economic
system is taking the form of a modified communism in many

so-called communist countries while so-called capitalist countries are moving in more socialist directions. To distinguish that from the eschatological views of Christianity and communism, both of which have been demythologized, I refer to Leslie Dewart's *Future of Belief* and *From Anathema to Dialog* by Garaudy, both published by Herder and Herder. Significant is new openness of communist figures to talk about the spiritual dimension in life and reality. The "fundamental" atheism of Marxism may turn out to be nonessential and temporary particularly with the rethinking among Christians about what we mean by God. Certainly the dialog should go on.

V. HAMILTON

It seems to me that the only thing necessary to say here is that there is no danger of communism in the North American continent today. What we need to enable ourselves and our young people today to survive in the future is more effective encounter with and dialog with communism as an ideology. This is what European, African, and Asian students get naturally, and we shelter our children, our young people, and even our college students from this. Anyone who does not know the power of communism from the inside cannot really be an effective citizen, either intellectually or practically.

21. Vietnam

I. JONES

War in Vietnam: We either ought to do whatever is necessary to clean it up quickly, or we should get out. It is wrong, indeed, it is wicked and criminal on the part of the President of the United States, to sacrifice the lives of American boys there in a half-hearted effort without clear-cut victory as its object. Decent men do not make human life an instrument of political expediency. If it is necessary to drop an atomic bomb on Hanoi in order to end the war and save the lives of our American boys, we should do so. The cowardice of our statesmen, so-called, and their groveling fear of Red China is nauseating.

II. HENRY

The war in Vietnam is one of the great tragedies of recent modern history. There can be little doubt that it was provoked by communist aggression, and that the United States responded in defense of victims of that aggression. Whether Vietnam was a theater that threatened vital American interests to the point where decisive counteraction was imperative is a matter for military debate. To the credit of the United States, it honored treaty commitments once these were made. The Christian has no right to urge unlimited use of destructive power even against an aggressor; the use of power must always be moralized in the context of justice. But a needlessly restricted response to North Vietnam not only expanded the toll of American losses and the suffering of the South Vietnamese people, but gave the communists repeated opportunity to wrest a propaganda advantage and to inflict continuing damage. Meanwhile it weakened the American economy, created expanding doubts about the rightness of the war, and weakened the will to win.

Christianity is a religion of peace. The biblical vision maintains that universal peace is messianic, hence a supernatural gift. The Christian religion emphasizes both that God wills justice and order through civil government, and that Christ offers new life to fallen men. While government — if just — has the power to announce and enforce the right, it cannot compel the right. And human history discloses that corruption sooner or later carries even the noblest nations into oblivion. Hence the Christian assault on a warring world consists first in the proclamation of the Prince of Peace.

The New Testament holds out no hope for the conversion of all men. It does not view regeneration, moreover, as establishing moral duty, but grounds ethical imperatives in the divine creation and preservation of men and nations. The commandments of God publish the standards by which God will judge both men and nations. Evangelical Christians emphasize that peace in a fallen world is a divine gift more than a human achievement, and that neither the power of prayer nor ministry of conversion should be neglected. It is righteousness that exalts a nation, while national pride and wickedness doom it. The tendency today is to seek a moral society while overlooking immoral man.

Most Christians (Mennonites are an exception), while recognizing the evil of war, consider a defensive war a just use of power. While the modern weapons of terrible destructive power multiply their anxieties over war, it is aggressor nations, rather than defender nations, that should be made to feel this terror.

III. MONTGOMERY

It is a hideous political mess — one of the worst in our nation's history. I spent a day at the 7th Annual Meeting of the American Society of Christian Ethics in January of 1966 listening to a bevy of political scientists speak to this issue in an effort to provide the facts needed so that ethical judgment on the war could be properly made. But the factual considerations are simply too muddy for simplistic ethical analysis. (For example, who is *really* the aggressor? Scripture will not countenance aggressive war, but unless we really know whether the communists got in there first *against the will* of the South Vietnamese — and who on earth knows what the will of the South Vietnamese *is* — how can we say that we, or the communists, are acting immorally?) I wish I could make a pat judgment either for (as the fundamentalists do) or against (as the liberals do), but I wonder if the mark of maturity here is steadfastly to do neither without more data. In the meantime, I must be "subordinate to the higher powers" of my own government (Rom 12) if I can't show that my country is acting immorally. *But* every day that sees equivocation from the White House (my friends in France call it lying), and confusion and bungling on the field, and men dying in the midst of ambiguities, my positive judgment on the whole business goes down another notch. Wars like this teach us a lesson, however: the lesson that the peoples of this globe are a remarkably stiff-necked lot, and there is not a nation or an individual who (in the words of the Church father and martyr Cyprian) can "stand upright amid the ruins of the world" apart from the sovereign grace of the Lord Christ.

IV. PIKE

I believe the United States should not have been in there or become so deeply involved. I believe that to prevent chaos we should stay in until there is a settlement. But we should be open to negotiation, and make clear that we will negotiate with *all* parties involved, including the NLF, to bring an end to this. I cannot believe killings and bombings are justified.

I don't believe that Vietnam wants to be part of the

Chinese hegemony. Over many centuries they have defeated the Chinese 19 times and also Genghis Kahn and his son and grandson; they still want their own independence. Doubtless they want to develop their own form of economy and government, which I think should be their business. If we are worried about the domino theory, we had better not push them to the point where they will have to open their borders to the Chinese to come in and support them and defend them. The North Vietnamese do not want the Chinese in Vietnam. They are keeping the Chinese out now and they estimate they will not need the Chinese unless there are two million American troops in the field, and I don't think that will happen. It would be better not to force them to have communist China move in the North, and therefore we should make clear we will stop the Hanoi bombing when we sit down to talk, and that we will include all parties, including NLF.

V. HAMILTON

I have been for several years involved in a number of rather ineffectual protest movements against not merely the escalation of this war but against the war itself. Now this ugly war is entering into the fabric of American life in a deeply tragic way. It is harming us psychologically as it hardens us morally to the ghastly things we're doing to a poor non-white people. America is losing such face as it had gained in its attempt to overcome racial discrimination and poverty in the earlier part of this decade. Indeed we are now a more fearful nation to most of the people in this world than either Russian or China could be.

I think if national communism in some form or another is the only way in which the Vietnamese nation can be organized, given order and security, then the people should be allowed to choose communism. We have no divine or human right to say to them, "Nay." I find the defenses of this war immoral and self-serving.

Index

Albright, W. F., on New Testament documents, 25
Altizer, Thomas J. J., and "death of God," 5; and God of Tillich, 11
American Council of Christian Churches, 77, 86
Anthropomorphism, 11
Anti-Semitism and Christian beliefs, 74; due to xenophobia, 74; Hamilton on, 74; Henry on, 72; Jones on, 71; Montgomery on, 73; Pike on, 74; result of sin, 73; un-Christian, 71
Auden, W. H., on hell, 52
Augustine, St., on Scripture, 32

Bible, attitudes toward, 6; doctrine of inspiration of, 35; errors in 34; Hamilton on, 35; Henry on, 31 f; inerrancy, 1, 31 f, 32 f; inerrancy, New Evangelical view, 2; inspiration of, 29 f, 31 f; Jones on, 29 f; Montgomery on, 32 f; Pike on, 34 f; and science and history, 32
Bob Jones University, 29
Bonhoeffer, Dietrich, on Christianity, 60
Brown, Robert McAfee, and spectrum, ix
Bultmann, Rudolph, and Virgin Birth, 24

Catholic, liberal, ix
Catholic Church, fundamentalist and, 2
Celibacy, Catholic Church and, 65; condemned, 61; may be preferred for larger freedom, 61; not required of all ministers, 61; sign of superiority, 61
Chastity, as option, 67
Christ, Second Coming, high orthodox belief in, 3
Church decorations and vestments, attitudes toward, 6

Communism, atheism may be temporary, 98; evil as atheistic and totalitarian, 97; fundamentalist and, 2; Hamilton on, 98; Henry on, 95 f; Jones on, 95; Montgomery on, 96 f; more dialog with, 98; no danger in North America, 98; not decisive enemy of gospel, 95; not worst of all evils, 97; Pike on, 97 f; satanic, 95
Confessional, on chart of attitudes, 6; estimates of numerical strength, 8
Confessional band of spectrum, denominational composition of, 7
Confessional position, description of, 3 f
Contraception, Catholic Church and, 65
Cox, Harvey, dialog with communists, 97; God, openness to the future, 13
Creeds, confessional emphasis on, 3

Dewart, Leslie, dialog with communists, 97; God is developmental, 13; and hellenization of dogma, 22; and omnipotence of God, 12
Divorce, and adultery, 62; attitudes toward, 6; Christian faith not against necessary, 63; fornication or adultery, grounds for, 61; Henry on, 61; Jones on, 61; as lesser of two evils, 62; Montgomery on, 62; Pike on, 62; and remarriage, right decision, 62
Doctrines, basic Christian, attitudes toward, 6

Eastern Orthodox, and divinity of Christ, 16; Nicene Creed, 10
Ecumenism, attitudes toward, 6; blasphemous, 75; compromises theology, 76; Hamilton on, 79; Henry on, 75 f; ignores evangelicals, 76;